GW00467851

Do-it-yourself

COHABITATION RIGHTS

LAW PACK™
GUIDE

Cohabitation Rights Guide
by Philippa Pearson

First edition 2001

© 2001 Law Pack Publishing Limited

Law Pack Publishing Limited
10-16 Cole Street
London SE1 4YH

www.lawpack.co.uk

Printed in Great Britain

ISBN: 1 902646 52 5
All rights reserved.

Crown copyright forms are reproduced with the permission of the
Controller of Her Majesty's Stationery Office.

This Law Pack Guide may not be reproduced in whole or in part in any form
without written permission from the publisher.

Important facts

This **Law Pack** Guide contains the information, instruction and examples of forms necessary for people who live together to enter into agreements with each other without a solicitor. This Guide is for use in England or Wales. It is not suitable for use in Scotland or Northern Ireland.

The information it contains has been carefully compiled from professional sources, but its accuracy is not guaranteed, as laws and regulations may change or be subject to differing interpretations.

Neither this nor any other publication can take the place of a solicitor on important legal matters. As with any legal matter, common sense should determine whether you need the assistance of a solicitor rather than rely solely on the information and forms in this **Law Pack** Guide.

We strongly urge you to consult a solicitor if:

- substantial amounts of money are involved;
- you do not understand the instructions or are uncertain how to complete and use a form correctly;
- what you want to do is not precisely covered by this Guide;
- trusts or business interests are involved.

Exclusion of Liability and Disclaimer

This book is sold with the understanding that neither the author nor the publisher is engaged in rendering legal advice. If legal advice is required, the services of a solicitor should be sought. The publisher and the author cannot in any way guarantee that the forms in this book are being used for the purposes intended and, therefore, assume no responsibility for their proper and correct use.

Whilst every effort has been made to ensure that this **Law Pack** Guide provides accurate and expert guidance, it is impossible to predict all the circumstances in which it may be used. Accordingly, the publisher, author, distributor, retailer and the solicitor who has approved the contents shall not be liable to any person or entity with respect to any loss or damage caused or alleged to be caused directly or indirectly by what is contained in or left out of this **Law Pack** Guide.

Contents

How to use this Law Pack Guide vii

Introduction ix

1   Preparing yourself 1

2   Finances 5

3   Setting up home 23

4   Children 39

5   Parental responsibility 43

6   Domestic violence 49

7   Wills and what happens if you die without one 53

8   Illness, incapacitation and death 59

9   Remedies in the event of separation or death 73

  Appendices 79

  Index 83

Contents

How to use this Law Pack Guide

This **Law Pack** Guide can help you achieve an important legal objective conveniently, efficiently and economically. Remember that it is important for you to use this guide properly if you are to avoid later difficulties.

Step-by-step instructions for using this guide:

1. Read this guide carefully. If after thorough examination you decide that your requirements are not met by this **Law Pack** Guide, or you do not feel confident about writing your own documents, consult a solicitor.

2. Throughout this Guide are examples of forms and agreements, original copies of which can be obtained from sources indicated in Appendix 1.

3. Once obtained, make several copies of the original forms for practice, for future use and for updates. You should also make copies of the completed forms. Create a record-keeping system for both sets of copies.

4. When completing a form, do not leave any section blank, unless instructed otherwise. If any section is inapplicable, write 'not applicable', 'none' or 'nil' to show you have not overlooked the section.

5. Always use a pen or type on legal documents; never use pencil.

6. Do not cross out or erase anything you have written on your final forms. If you do make an amendment, make sure everyone who is signing the document initials that amendment to show they have not overlooked it.

7. Always keep legal documents in a safe place and in a location known to your partner, family or solicitor.

In this Guide, for 'he', 'him', 'himself' and 'his', read 'he or she', 'him or her', 'himself or herself' and 'his or her'.

Cohabitation is chosen by an increasing number of people in Britain today. The proportion of all non-married women aged 18–49 who were cohabiting in Great Britain doubled between 1981 and 1997, to 25 per cent. More than one third of live births in Great Britain in 1997 occurred outside of marriage, which was more than four times the proportion in 1974. To this should be added the growing numbers of people in same-sex cohabiting relationships. This book is intended to help those people who live in a cohabiting relationship.

Introduction

I have been a family solicitor for many years and during that time I have worked with people from all walks of life: I have worked in the High Street with people who need public funding for their legal representation and in niche practices dealing with high net worth individuals. The law is the same for rich and poor and everybody who comes before it is treated equally – or are they? One of the most surprising distinctions at law is that of the differences that are drawn between those who are married and those who are unmarried. These distinctions never cease to amaze me and most of the clients that I see. There is often little or no logic or rationale to them.

I have dealt with many cases where somebody has given years to another person within a committed relationship and has been left, when their relationship has ended, either through sickness, death or separation, without protection. The law is meant to help people and to protect the vulnerable. However, the one area of the law which so rarely seems to do this is the law of cohabitation.

A large part of the reason why the law remains so unfair for those who cohabit is, I believe, because the majority of the population assume that they are protected by the law and that the act of living with someone automatically brings with it legal rights and obligations. Unfortunately, this is not the case.

The golden rule to remember is:

'There is no such thing as a common law wife or husband'

Prior to the introduction of the Marriage Act 1753, a form of common law marriage did exist in England and Wales. The situation then was not unlike the situation in England and Wales today: some people married in church, others entered into secret marriages and others were living together occasionally taking one surname to indicate that they were part of a domestic unit. Things began to go wrong in the 1690s with those who opted for these less formal arrangements, when the State attempted to raise money by putting a tax on marriages and later introduced stamp duty on marriage licences and certificates. The State was therefore clearly keen on seeing more formalised arrangements. In addition, the Church was becoming increasingly concerned about the number of children being born out of wedlock and the gentry were concerned about the confusion caused as to who would own property where there was no formal marriage. By contrast, amongst the more ordinary working population there was usually acceptance of a stable cohabiting relationship between a couple. Folk rituals had even developed which accompanied these less formal 'marriages', which took place without a member of the clergy being present. In some areas of Britain (especially the remoter areas such as Wales) it became customary for the 'bride' and 'groom' to jump a broomstick in order to signify that they were 'married' according to the common practice.

The 1753 Act put paid to these informal forms of marriage and the distinctions that the Act introduced between formal marriages and cohabitation remain in our law today, including in particular the difference in the way in which property rights are treated for those who are married and unmarried. Of course, for those who are in homosexual relationships, there is not even an old history of common law marriage to look at since people in those relationships have never been afforded any special rights.

As a result, whether you are in a homosexual or a heterosexual cohabiting relationship the law imposes no commitment or obligations between you save for certain limited obligations towards any children of the relationship. In the event of death, sickness or separation, therefore, the legal remedies are uncertain and complex.

This book tells you how to regularise your cohabiting relationship in the absence of clear help from the law. The different types of agreements that you can enter into in order to provide certainty and a solid framework for the way in which you deal with your arrangements are provided. Whilst these agreements should be treated as legally binding, this cannot always be guaranteed. However, in the event that they are not upheld by the Court they will always be considered good evidence of your intentions towards each other and as such should be valuable for both of you. In the majority of cases they will therefore provide a good clear framework as to what should happen in the event of death, sickness or separation so that legal intervention and large legal costs can be avoided in the future. It is still, however, always a good idea to take the advice of a specialist in this area of the law; when choosing one, take care they are indeed a specialist and that they are fully acquainted with the terms used in this book.

I should like to thank all my colleagues at The Family Law Consortium for their help in the preparation of this book, in particular Bradley Williams, Daniel Honeywell and Julie Secker. I am also indebted to Simon Adamyk for being an expert Counsel, as ever.

Philippa Pearson

Preparing
yourself

1

For many of those who live together unmarried, whether in heterosexual or same sex couples and whether or not they have children, there is a strong commitment to each other and to the family unit. Unfortunately, the law does not always reflect this and should such a relationship break down or death intervene, the couple or their family can find themselves in a sea of complex and unfair law, often without legal rights or remedies.

The cardinal rule is that, despite widespread belief to the contrary, **there is no such thing as a common law wife or husband**: however long you may have lived with someone, even if you have children together, you may still have no rights at all. To live together without a formal agreement as to what will happen if you separate, or one of you predeceases the other, is to leave yourself or your family in a very vulnerable or uncertain position, whether or not you are the one with good income or most of the capital in your relationship.

To protect your interests legally as partners, in this book we recommend that you enter the following agreements:

1. **The Living Together Agreement** – this is an agreement that deals with how you run your life, setting out for example who is responsible for the day-to-day care of any children and what arrangements exist for contact with them if the relationship breaks down, who will be responsible for the garden and who for the running of the house. A Living Together Agreement is not crucial and therefore if you do

not wish to regulate your personal life there is no reason why you should not ignore this agreement and move straight on to the Cohabitation or Financial Agreement referred to below. Terms covering issues of a personal nature, however, should not be included in a Financial Agreement because such terms would not be enforced by a court and may invalidate the agreement as a whole. If there are any personal issues you want to record, they should therefore go into the Living Together Agreement document. See chapter 3 which discusses the Living Together Agreement and gives a precedent.

2. **The Cohabitation** or **Financial Agreement** – this is an agreement that deals with the financial structure of your relationship. It can include how you own your home, what is to happen to it if your relationship breaks down, what provision you will make for each other and the children on death, how you will share the bills, etc. Once such an agreement is signed as a deed it will become a binding contract between the two of you. It is usually wise to combine this agreement with the making of Wills and, if you own property together, a trust deed. See chapter 3, which discusses the Cohabitation Agreement and sets out a precedent.

3. When you purchase a property it can often be a good idea to enter into a **trust deed** which sets out clearly what will happen to the property in the event of your relationship breaking down or one of you pre-deceasing the other. For details of the factors to be considered and for a precedent, see chapter 3.

4. If you have children you may wish to enter into a **Parental Responsibility Agreement**. Chapter 5 discusses in detail how this Agreement works and provides a precedent.

5. In case one of you becomes incapacitated (e.g. after an accident), you may wish to give your partner an **Enduring Power of Attorney** so they can continue to run your affairs; in addition you may wish to draw up a **Living Will** stating what should happen in the event that you are on a life support machine. For full details of this and precedents, see chapter 8.

6. Death happens to us all and as part of your Cohabitation or Financial Agreement, you may wish to agree that you should make **Wills** to reflect what you intend to happen to your property in the event of your deaths. For details on this see chapter 7 'Wills, and what happens if you die without one'.

Chapter 9, 'Remedies in the event of separation or death' discusses the legal remedies that you have in the event that your relationship breaks down and you do not have an agreement that is binding between the two of you.

This book cannot guarantee that the Cohabitation Agreement that you reach will be upheld by the courts. However, providing you have told each other the truth about your financial circumstances, neither of you has exerted unfair or undue influence over the other and you have both taken independent legal advice, then there is no reason why your agreement should not be upheld. By preparing your own deed you can help to minimise your legal costs. Furthermore, the agreement will always provide good evidence of what your intentions are towards each other and your children – evidence which is usually, sadly, lacking.

It is considered sensible that couples review and if necessary renew their contracts in the event that significant changes occur in their relationship, e.g. the birth of a child, redundancy, severe illness or disability. It is then more likely that the courts will uphold them and will treat them as being binding.

The Law Commission (a body set up by the Lord Chancellor to consider areas of the law that require reform) announced in 1995 that it would publish 'next year' its thoughts of changing the law in relation to home ownership. At the time of going to press, they have yet to report. Until the law is reformed, therefore, people in committed relationships who wish to be certain of their rights and wish to protect themselves should enter into the type of formal agreements that we refer to in this book, rather than to leave themselves at the mercy of the law. It goes without saying that it is better to work out exactly the arrangements between you when all is well, and to record it in formal documentation, rather than to wait until things are going wrong.

Mediation

If you have a problem which you want to resolve together without going to court, or if you are finding it difficult to agree upon the terms of your Living Together Agreement or Cohabitation Agreement, then consider mediation. It comprises a meeting or a series of meetings, usually between a couple and a mediator, the aim of which is to help the couple to find a solution to issues that have arisen between them. These issues can deal with many matters, such as arrangements for children, financial arrangements, dividing up property or other practical issues connected with separation.

If the issue is arrangements for children, then the mediator will usually help the couple to decide what is best for the children and how and when they should tell them. The mediator will also encourage the couple to concentrate on their children's needs and to consider their wishes and feelings when making arrangements for their future.

If the problems that the couple are experiencing relate to financial arrangements, the mediator(s) will usually ask them to fill out a form giving full details of their income and outgoings, assets, loans or other debts, so that an exchange of details regarding their respective financial circumstances can take place and thereafter can help the couple to try to reach an agreement concerning all financial matters.

Whilst in mediation, the mediators can give the couple general information about the law and the way that the legal system works, but they cannot give individual advice about their legal rights. Often, therefore, it can be a good idea to take independent legal advice from a solicitor both during mediation and at the end to make sure that any agreement reached is suitable. Often, a solicitor is also needed at the end of mediation to draw up an order for the court in order to formalise any agreement reached.

Mediation usually takes place in a private and informal setting. As part of the process, the mediator(s) will usually help the couple to listen to each other, to understand each other's needs and concerns and, thereafter, to find a solution to the issues between them. The mediator will always be neutral so will neither tell the couple what to do nor will take sides; however, they will often share ideas with a couple and help a couple to explore different solutions.

Mediation is confidential because it is entered into by a couple on a voluntary basis and is outside the parameters of the courts. Therefore any proposals that are discussed in mediation cannot be referred to outside the mediation setting unless something is said during mediation to the effect that a child or an adult has suffered significant harm or is at risk of doing so. In these rare circumstances the mediator(s) would then have to make sure that the police or social services were told.

In order for mediation to be successful, it is essential that both parties are prepared to share all their relevant information with the other and that they do not feel threatened or pressurised.

Mediation can help to reach an agreement and, in particular, one that you should feel you 'own' (as opposed to an arrangement that is foisted upon you by a judge). It can also help to reduce tension, hostility and misunderstanding. A by-product of this can often be an improvement in communication, which can be particularly important if the couple have children and need to co-operate over their care and upbringing for many years to come. Other advantages of mediation include:

- A reduction in the feelings of hostility.

- Mutually agreed outcomes (rather than outcomes imposed by the court or negotiated by others).

- Greater focus on the needs of the children.

- Confidentiality.

- Outcomes that are more likely to be implemented.

- Cost-effectiveness (mediation is cheaper than litigating disputes).

- Opportunity for legal advice running alongside, but independent of, mediation.

- It is voluntary – both parties have to agree to attend.

- The couple retain control of areas for which solutions need to be found.

The UK College of Family Mediators' address is in Appendix 2.

2

Finances

The law relating to married couples

When a married couple's relationship breaks down, their financial arrangements are regulated by Act of Parliament: the Matrimonial Causes Act 1973. This Act sets out the factors that the court should consider and there are thousands of decided cases that have helped judges and legal practitioners interpret how the Act should be applied to people's individual circumstances.

The law relating to cohabitants ——

Unfortunately, the law relating to people who live together is not so simple. There is no Act of Parliament to regulate how their financial affairs should be dealt with on the breakdown of their relationship, however long they have lived together, whatever promises they have made to each other and whether or not they have children. The law that relates to them is the same as applies to people living together without an intimate relationship, e.g. two platonic friends or two distant relatives. The law that relates to engaged couples is slightly different, much of it being set out in the Married Women's Property Act 1882; it is outside the scope of this book and you are therefore advised to take legal advice if you are an engaged couple, especially if your financial affairs are complex or you are wealthy.

When the relationship breaks down

If a couple who live together have not entered into a Cohabitation Agreement concerning their financial arrangements then, in the event that their relationship breaks down, the court has to look at the available evidence to decide whether they come within one of the complex doctrines that are found in 'equity' and which are set out below. Put simply, equity is the court's search for justice. The law of equity is not found in an Act of Parliament, but in case law going back hundreds of years. When he was Master of the Rolls, Lord Denning was keen on extending and developing the doctrine of equity in order to produce what he saw as a just result in cases where legal ownership seemed to ignore justice. Although the law relating to cohabitants is messy and unfair in many instances, without Lord Denning it would be much worse and we therefore have a lot to thank him for. Equity means that the court will look behind who *legally* owns something (e.g. the person who is registered as the owner of a property at the Land Registry – see also chapter 3 'Setting up home') and at who *should* have an interest in the property and what that interest is; this is often referred to as a 'beneficial interest'.

Property and capital

Legal ownership

There are two ways of owning a property (i.e. a house or flat) – either 'legally' or 'beneficially' as referred to above.

The legal ownership of a property relates to whom is shown to be the owner of the property either at the Land Registry or on the title deeds. How a property is legally owned between a couple can therefore often be the end of the story; for example, if a property is held in one person's sole name and the other person cannot show that they have a beneficial interest in the property by applying one of the equitable doctrines set out below, then the legal owner will retain their 100 per cent interest in the property, however long the other person may have lived with them. It is therefore important that when you buy a property you instruct the solicitor who acts on your purchase to reflect in the legal documentation how you intend to own the property (see chapter

3). If the property is owned jointly on a beneficial basis, then the owners are either:

i)   'joint tenants'; or

ii)   'tenants in common'.

If the couple own the property as joint tenants then they are deemed to have equal and indivisible shares in the property (subject to any redistribution of their interest in the property because of the application of the equitable doctrines referred to below). This means that if one of them dies before the other, then the share of the deceased will pass automatically to the survivor under the right of survivorship and will not pass according to the terms of their Will or the law of intestacy. If a couple wish the property to be owned equally and for their share in the property to pass automatically to the surviving partner upon their death, then this is the way in which the property should be held.

If the joint owners of the property are tenants in common, then the couple have divisible shares in the property which may or may not be equal. If one of them dies before the other, the share of the deceased will not pass automatically to the survivor, but instead according to the terms of the deceased's Will, or the law of intestacy if they do not have a Will. This is usually the most appropriate way for people who live together to own a property, particularly if there are other relatives (e.g. children) whom they would like to benefit from their share in the property in the event of their death. See chapter 3, 'Setting up home', for details of the instructions that should be given to the conveyancing solicitor when a property is purchased. It is a good idea for couples who own a property as tenants in common to enter into a deed of trust which records the terms on which they own the property, e.g. when it should be sold and how the proceeds of sale should be divided.

Beneficial interests (and equitable doctrines)

Express trusts

If a couple do not intend to own a property equally or intend to own it as tenants in common or, alternatively, they want to have the property legally registered in one person's name but held jointly between the two of them on a beneficial basis, then they should instruct the solicitor on the purchase of their property to prepare a deed of trust which will state exactly how the property is owned and by whom. This is then referred to as an express trust because the details are written and are therefore 'express' or clear. This is dealt with in more detail in chapter 3, 'Setting up home'.

Resulting trusts

This is the doctrine that can be applied to calculate somebody's interest in a property by reference to their *actual* contribution to a property, irrespective of how the legal title to the property is held, for example:

i) if the property is held jointly, but one party has made a larger financial contribution than the other, then they may be able to claim more than 50 per cent interest in the property using the resulting trust doctrine; or

ii) if the property is held in one party's sole name but the other person has made a financial contribution to it, then that person may be able to claim an interest by way of resulting trust.

To calculate a resulting trust, the court would calculate the percentage value in the net proceeds of sale or the value of the property which relates to the *actual* financial contribution made to it. For example, if a property is held in Tony's sole name and is worth £100,000 and Val has made a contribution towards it of £30,000, then Val may claim she has a 30 per cent interest in the property by way of a resulting trust.

Mortgages make the calculation of a resulting trust more complex. This is because if someone's name is on a mortgage, then, whether or not they have actually paid monies towards that mortgage, they are said to have contributed to the value of that mortgage on the property. This is rather complex and can be best explained by the following example:

1980 – Tony and Val buy Fairacres for £100,000 in their joint names with Tony providing a £20,000 deposit. The repayment mortgage is for £80,000 in Tony and Val's joint names. Tony pays all the mortgage payments.

2000 – Fairacres is now worth £200,000, with £60,000 of the mortgage having been paid off by Tony, leaving £20,000 outstanding.

Tony wants to claim more than 50 per cent interest in the property by way of resulting trust.

1980 – purchase price = £100,000

Tony		Val	
Deposit –	£20,000	Deposit –	nil
Mortgage –	£40,000	Mortgage –	£40,000
Total:	**£60,000**	**Total:**	**£40,000**

So at the time of the purchase in 1980, Tony could claim a 60 per cent interest and Val a 40 per cent interest, by way of resulting trust.

2000 – By now, Tony has paid off £60,000 of the £80,000 mortgage so he might argue that he has contributed the following:

Tony		Val	
Deposit –	£20,000	Mortgage -	£40,000
Mortgage – Adjustment to take into account mortgage paid off	£40,000 £20,000	Val's adjustment to take into account mortgage payments	–£20,000
Total:	**£80,000**	**Total:**	**£20,000**

Accordingly, Tony may claim he has an 80 per cent interest in the property and Val has a 20 per cent interest calculated as follows:

Fairacres now worth	£200,000	
Outstanding mortgage of	£20,000	
Total equity:	£180,000	
Tony 80% of £180,000 =		£144,000
Val 20% of £180,000 =		£36,000

The above example is done on the basis that Tony and Val have a repayment mortgage, which is a mortgage that pays off both the capital that has been borrowed and the interest. However, a lot of couples have an endowment mortgage and that makes the calculations much more complex, because it will mean that Tony has been paying the interest only on the mortgage, but has not actually made any inroads into the capital that is owing on the mortgage. Tony would obviously want to claim that all the interest payments he has been making over the years should be taken into account, but there is no hard and fast formula for working out how this would be calculated. In other words, if Tony has paid interest payments of £25,000, he cannot necessarily claim a credit of £25,000 although clearly he should be given some credit for doing this. This is one of the examples of how the law relating to cohabitants can be such a mess; the law is unclear and in many cases the courts have done contrary things, and so one cannot say with certainty what any future decision is going to be.

Matters might be made even more complicated by the fact that Val has always paid the building insurance and certainly, because this is a contribution towards the property, it would be taken into account when trying to calculate what the value of Tony and Val's beneficial interests are in the property. But if Val's money has always gone towards such things as the food shopping, the cost of holidays, child care and other matters that do not relate to the actual fabric of the building, then even though she may have paid more money than Tony over the years into the household pot, she may find that the court does not take into account these contributions at all and that she still ends up with a less than 50 per cent interest in the property (although see the equitable doctrine of proprietary estoppel below which could be of some help).

If the property is a council property bought under The Right to Buy Scheme, the person who had the right to buy is treated as having contributed towards the purchase price of the property the same value as the value of the discount obtained under the Scheme.

Although a resulting trust is probably the easiest way of calculating somebody's interest in a property by way of an equitable doctrine, it can be seen that it is by no means clear and simple. It can lead to substantial legal costs being incurred if couples have to fall back on this type of calculation to work out what they both own. Furthermore, the court will not apply the resulting trust doctrine if there is evidence (i.e. an agreement) that this is not what the couple intended. If Fairacres is registered in joint names therefore, Tony may find the court considers Val has a 50 per cent interest in the property by applying one of the other equitable doctrines, such as proprietary estoppel (see below). Moreover, the law is such that if the available documentation shows that the property was conveyed into joint names and there is no evidence of other agreements then the courts will still declare Tony and Val to have a 50 per cent interest in the property. If this happens and Tony has spent more money than Val on the property, e.g. by repairing or extending it, the only way he might get his money back (but no more) would be by applying the doctrine of equitable accounting (see below). Far better therefore that couples should regulate the ownership of the property by entering into a trust deed (see chapter 3, 'Setting up home') and to enter into a Cohabitation Agreement to regulate their ownership of any other assets/investments they may have.

The constructive trust

In order to find a constructive trust, a court will look for:

i)   some sort of agreement or common intention between the couple, whether express or implied that the property was to be held jointly and how it was to be held; or

ii)   a promise or a declaration made by the person who has the legal title to the property to the other person, usually that the other person had a beneficial interest in the property; and

iii) the person who is not a legal title holder and is claiming the beneficial interest did something to their detriment as a result of the agreement or common intention or as a result of the promise or representation made by the legal title holder.

The courts have declared that the following things are examples of detriment and as a result have given the person claiming the beneficial interest an interest in the property:

•   giving up a council tenancy;

- helping to renovate the property on the strength of an agreement that if they did so they would gain a beneficial interest in it;

- making substantial contributions to household expenses on the strength of an implied promise that as a result they would get a beneficial interest in the property.

Accordingly, the person who has paid such things as the shopping bills, child care, holidays, etc., but has not actually paid anything towards the property, may be able to claim that they have a beneficial interest in the family home by applying the constructive trust doctrine. However, a lot of people in this situation have failed to establish a constructive trust. This is because the courts have made it clear that the fact that a couple pool their resources is insufficient on its own to create a constructive trust. This is because there must also be evidence that the couple had an agreement or a common intention. Of course, the legal title owner is often going to argue that there was no such common intention and as a result, the person in the couple who did not directly contribute to the property may end up with nothing at all.

'Proprietary estoppel'

In order to establish a beneficial interest by applying this doctrine, the court must be convinced of the following:

i) that the person claiming the beneficial interest was mistaken as to their legal rights (usually they would have thought they either had an interest in the property or were building one up); and

ii) that person must have acted to their detriment in reliance of that mistaken belief; and

iii) that the other person must have known the truth about the claimant's legal right; and

iv) that the legal owner must also be aware of the claimant's mistaken belief; and

v) that the legal title holder must have encouraged the claimant to act to their detriment.

Unless all of the above elements (i)–(v) are present (except perhaps (iii) in certain circumstances) then there will be no estoppel and so it can be very difficult for somebody to claim proprietory estoppel unless they can prove each one of the above factors.

For example, if Tony purchases Fairacres in his sole name but says to Val, 'this property is yours as much as mine' (knowing or believing that it isn't) and Val (with Tony's encouragement) therefore decorates it, refurbishes it, landscapes the garden and pays for all the shopping and household bills, then Tony would be 'estopped' from denying Val any interest in the property and Val will obviously be trying to claim that she has a 50 per cent interest in the property. As with resulting trusts and constructive trusts, however, there is no simple formula to calculate precisely what interest Val would have in the property (it cannot be guaranteed that she would establish as much as 50 per cent) and accordingly, enormous legal costs can be incurred trying to establish this.

Whilst the courts try to be as fair as they can when considering a case of proprietary estoppel, they will only give the claimant the bare minimum required for justice to be done.

Equitable accounting

Equitable accounting is a process whereby if someone has contributed extra money to a property then they can claim back that money. Unlike a resulting trust, however, the contributor cannot claim back the value of the repairs they have carried out. Therefore, if Tony were to build a conservatory at Fairacres which costs £10,000 but which enhanced the value of Fairacres by £20,000 he would only be able to claim back £10,000 under the system of equitable accounting. Despite this, it would be useful for Tony to rely on equitable accounting if any of the following instances applied:

- he could not establish a resulting trust or other equitable doctrine, e.g. if there was no common intention or agreement.

- the property market has actually gone down and whilst he may have spent £10,000 on improving Fairacres, the value of Fairacres has only gone up by £5,000.

An example of equitable accounting is as follows:

Tony and Val buy Fairacres in their joint names for	£100,000
Tony builds conservatory at cost	£10,000
Fairacres sold for	£150,000
Tony receives	£150,000
divided by 2	= £75,000
Conservatory	£10,000
	= £85,000
Val receives	£65,000

The doctrine of equitable accounting also takes into account the following, which are often useful arguments to use when trying to establish how much one party should pay the other in the event that a relationship breaks down:

1. Val left the property on 1 April 2001. She immediately stopped paying the mortgage. Tony can therefore claim Val's half-share of any capital payments he makes towards the repayment of the mortgage during her absence.

2. If Val was asked to leave by Tony, or had to leave because of his behaviour towards her, she may be able to argue that she should not pay her half-share of the capital repayments towards the mortgage until a reasonable time has elapsed for Tony to sell the property or to get in a lodger (3-6 months, say).

3. Val could claim from Tony occupational rent for the fact that he is using her half-share in the property now that she has gone. Usually this is calculated by reference to the one half of the interest element of the mortgage payments. However, if the mortgage is low Val could argue that it should be one half of the market rental value of the property.

4. Tony could claim from Val half of any payments that he makes towards the building of the property, e.g. buildings insurance, essential maintenance and Council Tax.

As can be seen from the above doctrines, therefore, by far the most simple and effective way of regulating your financial circumstances is to enter into a Cohabitation Agreement, because this provides clear evidence of what you intended. It is also important to ensure that when you purchase a property together your conveyancing solicitor has clear instructions as to how you intend to own the property and is instructed to prepare the correct legal documentation (see chapter 3, 'Setting up home').

Severing a joint tenancy

Severance is the process by which you convert a joint tenancy into a tenancy in common. If you have therefore already purchased your property in joint names as joint tenants and you wish to sever the tenancy this is a relatively simple procedure: a precedent for severing the tenancy is provided on the following pages for registered and unregistered land, with a 'without prejudice' covering letter that should go with it. This should be sent by the person who is severing the tenancy to the other tenant or joint owner. It is not crucial that the person receiving the notice of severance acknowledges it by signing the duplicate copy; however, if they do so, then there is clear evidence that they have received the notice of severance. You can, however, prove severance by ensuring that the notice of severance is served by registered post. There is a presumption of the newly created tenancy in common being in equal shares. If the person serving the notice wants to reserve the right to argue that they have a more than 50 per cent share in the property therefore, they should serve the notice of severance without prejudice to their claim that they own more than 50 per cent – see the precedent covering letter.

There is nothing that the party who receives the notice of severance can do to stop the severance. This is because it takes place automatically on service of the notice.

In order to fill out the notice of severance you will see that you need the title number of your property if it is registered at

Example 'without prejudice' covering letter for Notice of Severance of a joint tenancy

23 Chankly Bore
Zemmery Fidd
Dorset

12 March 2001

Valerie Mary Judd
c/o Jumblies
Dong Road
Lear
Dorset

SENT BY REGISTERED POST

Dear Valerie

Please find enclosed Notice of Severance of our joint tenancy on 23 Chankly Bore which I am sending to you without prejudice to the fact that I may contend that I own more than a 50% beneficial interest in the property.

I urge you to take legal advice upon the contents of this letter.

Yours sincerely

TONY ARTHUR SMITH

Enc: Notice of Severance

Example Notice of Severance of a joint tenancy

NOTICE OF SEVERENCE OF JOINT TENANCY
(registered and unregistered land)

Concerning the property known as 23 Chankly Bore, Zemmery Fidd, Dorset (herein called **'the Property'**)

From   **TONY ARTHUR SMITH** of the Property (hereinafter called **'the Donor'**)

To   **VALERIE MARY JUDD** of the Property (hereinafter called **'the Donee'**)

The Donor **HEREBY GIVES NOTICE** to the Donee that any joint tenancy in equity which may exist between them in respect of the Property is hereby severed and henceforth the said Property is held **IN TRUST** for the Donor and Donee as tenants in common, but **Without Prejudice** to any claims the Donor might have made or may make to the effect that his share in the Property is more than 50%.

Dated this   day of   2001

Signed ………………………...............…
     TONY ARTHUR SMITH

I acknowledge receipt of the Notice of which this is a copy

Dated this   day of   2001

Signed ………………………...............…
     VALERIE MARY JUDD

HM Land Registry. If you telephone the general enquiry section of HM Land Registry (on 020 7917 8888) they will give you details of where your property is likely to be registered and which Land Registry you should be dealing with. That Land Registry will then assist you with the application to find out the title number under which your property is registered.

Once the tenancy has been severed you should then notify the Land Registry in writing of the severance giving them full details of how it occurred. They will then note the Land Registry entry for your property accordingly.

If your property is unregistered then there will be no Land Registry title number for you to find out and it will simply be sufficient for you to put in the full address of the property. Again the notice of severance should be served by registered post and you then protect your property by attaching the notice of severance and evidence of it having been served to the title deeds.

Personal possessions

When couples live together, the person who buys an item tends to own it, unless it was a gift to the other or it was intended by the couple that they would jointly own it. This is the case even when the item has been purchased out of a joint account, and even if it is the other party who has put most of the monies into that account. Any items that are purchased with the intention that they will be owned jointly are owned jointly and, of course, there will then be difficulties deciding who is to have the item or whether it is to be sold. In order to avoid problems with this it is far better to enter into a Cohabitation Agreement which deals with the ownership of such items. Any items that are inherited or given to one party during the relationship belong to that party and are not owned jointly.

Income

Another important thing to remember is that for couples who live together unmarried, on the breakdown of their relationship one party does not have any legal obligation to maintain the other and to pay them any income (i.e. maintenance). Indeed, even if they went to court, the court could not make an order that one of them should pay maintenance to the other. In the Cohabitation Agreement, however, you could agree that one of you would pay maintenance to the other in the event of your relationship breaking down. This can be important if one of you does not have much income and there is insufficient capital to make up for that loss of previous joint income. Beware, however: there could be difficulties enforcing these payments. See the paragraph below for maintenance (i.e. child support) for children.

Child support

Although one party in a couple cannot claim maintenance from the other, if there are children then child support can be claimed from the parent who is known as the 'absent parent' (i.e. the parent with whom the child does not live on a day-to-day basis). The Child Support Agency assesses and enforces the payment of child support. The present formula for its calculation is very complex and would take up far too many pages in this book to spell out in detail. However, the Government is currently considering introducing a simpler formula which may come into effect in 2001. It is currently being proposed that an absent parent will pay 15 per cent of his net income to one child, 20 per cent of his net income to two children or 25 per cent of his net income to three children. The Government has decided that there will be a cap so that no absent parent will pay more than £15,000, £20,000 or £25,000 (depending on the number of children) by way of child support. The calculation of net income will be based upon gross income less tax, National Insurance and pension contributions. If you do not wish to involve the Child Support Agency you could agree a level of maintenance between you and have it enshrined in a deed (see chapter 9). There may be some difficulties in enforcing such a deed, but if you trust each other, and do not want to involve the Child Support Agency in your affairs, this may be a good way of regulating the arrangements you want to have for the support of children.

Setting up home 3

Buying a property together and entering into a trust deed

When you decide to buy a property together you should first consider how that property is going to be held legally. First, is it appropriate that it should be held in one person's sole name?

Property held in one person's sole name

If the property is only to be legally held in one person's sole name, the couple should be clear as to what the other person's interest in the property will be. It may be that you will decide that the other person should have a beneficial interest in the property and if so, this should be reflected in a trust deed which lies behind the legal title. Your conveyancing solicitor can be asked to draft this trust deed and the bare bones of it can also be set out in your Cohabitation Agreement. The trust deed may include provision for how one of you will buy out the other in the event that your relationship breaks down. The trust deed will then specifically deal with your interests in the property and, as it is a standard legal document, will be binding on you both. The Cohabitation Agreement deals with matters other than property and since there is always a risk that it may not be upheld, it is wise to execute these two separate documents.

Because the trust deed lies behind the legal title, it is important that any person who purchases the legal title has notice of it. Most properties are registered at the Land Registry and therefore if there is a trust deed, the person who has the beneficial interest under the trust deed will usually protect their interest by registering what is known as a 'restriction' against the title to the property on the Land Registry in a form C1 or C2. It is more difficult to protect that person if the property is not registered. In that case, the person with the beneficial interest under the trust deed can only protect their interest by registering their interest at the Land Charges Registry in Portsmouth (on 0123 9276 8888). (The Land Charges Registry are helpful and will provide up-to-date forms.) A simple example of a trust deed is shown opposite.

Owning the property in joint names

There are two ways of owning a property jointly (as already discussed in chapter 2). The first is as 'joint tenants' which means that on the face of it you each have an equal interest in the property and if one of you predeceases the other, the share of the deceased passes automatically to the survivor under the principle known as 'the right of survivorship' and not according to the deceased's Will (whatever it may say) or the law of intestacy.

The other way of owning a property jointly is as 'tenants in common'. If you own a property as tenants in common then you do not necessarily have equal shares and, in any event, your shares are separate, which means that if one of you predeceases the other the share of the deceased does not pass automatically to the survivor but instead, according to the terms of the deceased's Will or the law of intestacy, as appropriate. See chapter 7 for further details on this.

When you purchase a property, therefore, you should discuss with your conveyancing solicitor whether you wish to own the property as joint tenants or as tenants in common. If you intend to hold it as tenants in common you should discuss with your conveyancing solicitor whether you should also enter into a trust deed in order that you can deal in detail with the following issues:

- The exact percentage of your beneficial interests in the property.

- What is to happen in the event that your relationship breaks down. Who is to buy out the other and how the value of the property is to be calculated. Whether one party will be

Example trust deed

THIS DEED OF TRUST is made the   day of

BETWEEN:

[   ] of [   ] (hereinafter called the Trustee)
of the one part and [   ] and [   ] both of [   ]
(hereinafter called the Beneficiaries) of the other part

WHEREAS:

(1)   The Beneficiaries purchased the freehold property known as [   ]
as registered at HM Land Registry with title absolute under title number [   ]
(hereinafter called the Property) on [   ] and held the Property as joint tenants
in law and equity

(2)   On the date hereof the legal estate in the Property was transferred by the Beneficiaries to the Trustee

(3)   By a mortgage deed (hereinafter called the Mortgage) made on the date hereof the Trustee charged the
Property to [   ] with payment of all sums payable or to become payable by
her to [   ]

(4)   The parties hereto have agreed that the Property shall be held on the trusts hereinafter appearing

NOW THIS DEED WITNESSETH as follows:

1.   The Trustee declares that she holds the Property on trust to sell the same with power to postpone sale
and shall hold the net proceeds on trust for the Beneficiaries as joint tenants in law and equity / tenants in
common in equal shares

2.   The parties hereto will jointly make all payments of capital and interest under the Mortgage to
[   ] or their successors in title

IN WITNESS whereof the parties hereto have executed this document as their deed the day and year first
before written

Signed as a Deed
By the said
[   ]
in the presence of:

Signed as a Deed
By the said
[   ]
in the presence of:

allowed to vacate the property and if so, who will then be responsible for paying the outgoings and the mortgage on the property.

- Under what circumstances will the property be sold.

- What you intend to happen to the property in the event of death.

- Who is to pay for outgoings relating to the property, e.g. buildings insurance and repairs.

- How you will agree the method by which improvements, repairs, etc. will be carried out.

- How you will take into account any failure to pay any of the items referred to in the trust deed, i.e. will there be a re-calculation of your respective beneficial interests in the property.

- Many other issues besides.

Living Together Agreement and precedent

The Living Together Agreement is a document in which a couple can record any moral or lifestyle issues that are non-legal. It can therefore deal with many issues, including the following:

- Who is to have responsibility for cleaning the family home.

- Who is to have responsibility for cooking for the family.

- What nights each of the couple will be in the home and how many outside interests they are to have and how many nights this can take them away from the home.

- How they intend to bring up the children, giving basic principles of discipline, religious upbringing or the type of schooling the children should have.

- Who they will turn to in the event of relationship difficulties, e.g. to Relate or to a religious organisation.

- What restrictions they place on each other, e.g. Tony will not criticise Val's mother, Val's mother will not come and stay for any longer than three days at a time and on no more than three separate occasions in a year.

- How the house is to be run, e.g. Tony will keep his room tidy and Val will not enter it unless specifically asked to.

The above list is by no means exhaustive. An example of a simple precedent is provided on the following pages to which you can add as many clauses as you like. The main thing to bear in mind, however, is that this is not a legally binding agreement – it is just to record the way in which you intend to live together. It is also not crucial that you enter into an agreement such as this – you can simply move onto the Cohabitation Agreement in the next section if all you wish to do is regulate your financial affairs. You must, however, take care that you do not include any financial arrangements in this Living Together Agreement because if you do, it is unlikely that it will be upheld by the court because of the other non-legal issues that are included in the document.

Cohabitation Agreement and precedent

The Cohabitation Agreement is the agreement in which you set out the financial obligations you want to have between you. It should therefore cover, for instance, the following:

- Who will pay what outgoings on your home (e.g. electricity bills, water bills, etc).

- How repairs and improvements to your home will be agreed.

- How those repairs and improvements will be funded.

- What will be the circumstances in which your home will be sold; and how the sale proceeds are to be divided/used.

- How any mortgage arrears might be met.

- How you will operate any joint accounts.

- How you will operate any joint credit cards.

Example precedent for a Living Together Agreement

THIS LIVING TOGETHER AGREEMENT is made between:

Tony Arthur Smith ('Tony') of 23 Chankly Bore, Zemmery Fidd, Dorset and Valerie Mary Judd ('Val') of 23 Chankly Bore, Zemmery Fidd, Dorset

(1)   We cohabit/intend to cohabit by which we mean:

that we will live together as a family unit and hold ourselves out as being a family;
that we will share our lives together;
we will support each other emotionally;
we will be honest to each other;
we will be sexually faithful to each other.

(2)   We have the following children:

(a)   Alfred Smith;
(b)   Zara Judd;
(c)   Austin Smith-Judd.

(3)   Alfred is Tony's child by his first marriage and Zara is a child by Valerie's previous relationship. It is agreed that they are to be treated as children of the family unit and that both Tony and Val can discipline each other's child, as appropriate but under no circumstances may they use physical force against the other's child.

(4)   In the case of Austin, he is the child of both Tony and Val and it is agreed that they each have equal rights, duties and responsibilities towards Alfred which is reflected in the Parental Responsibility Agreement that Val and Tony have entered into dated 3rd March 2001.

(5)   Val understands that Tony does not get on well with her mother and likewise Tony understands that Val likes her to come and stay, particularly to help with the care of the children during the school holidays. As a compromise therefore, it is agreed that Val's mother will not come and stay for any longer than 3 days at a time and on no more than 3 separate occasions in each year. On each occasion, Val must ask Tony at least 2 weeks prior to her mother's arrival if her mother may come and Tony will not unreasonably withhold his consent.

(6)   Val understands that Tony is passionate about Bedford United. Tony recognises however that when he goes to matches this creates additional work for Val who is left to look after the children on her own. Tony therefore agrees that he will not go to any more than 4 matches in any one season. The cost of attending those matches will be borne solely by Tony and will not be paid for out of the joint account. Tony will not stay overnight at his friend Bill's house after attending these matches.

(7)   Tony appreciates that Val is a member of the Elim Pentecostal Church and he will not prevent Val from taking the children to Church every Sunday morning. Likewise, Val will not pressurise Tony into accompanying them.

(8)   In the event that Tony and Val have difficulties in their relationship they both promise to discuss them with each other at the earliest opportunity. Should either Tony or Val wish to refer their difficulties to an organisation, counsellor or therapist the other will not withhold their agreement to attend at least the first 3 sessions with that organisation/individual.

(Continued on next page)

(9)   Val and Tony have agreed that all of the children, Alfred, Zara and Austin will attend the Rudolf Steiner School in Borset for as long as Tony's mother is willing to pay their respective school fees.

(10)   Val acknowledges that Tony has higher standards of cleanliness and home neatness than she does. Commencing the 1st April 2001 Val and then Tony shall, on a monthly basis, alternate as the inspector of household work for cleanliness and neatness. On the month when Tony is inspector, Val will conform to his standards and Tony will conform to the standards set by Val during her month.

(11)   Tony will not play his saxaphone after 9.30pm in the evening and on no more than 3 nights a week.

Since a living together agreement is not a legally binding document, you can then put in numbered paragraph concerning any matters you consider appropriate. Issues commonly covered include the following:

Children

(a)   registering the birth;

(b)   the child's surname;

(c)   care of the child including discipline;

(d)   religion;

(e)   expected education;

(f)   childcare

(g)   personal relations

(h)   contraception

(i)   sexual relations

(j)   marriage – the prospect of

(k)   housekeeping

(l)   housework

Signed

....

Tony Arthur Smith

Signed

....

Valerie Mary Judd

Dated ....

- How you will own your savings.

- What the terms of your Wills will be in relation to each other.

- Who will be responsible for any children's school fees.

- What will be any agreement you may have regarding entering into an Enduring Power of Attorney or a Living Will.

- How you will own possessions.

- Whether the occupier can invite a new partner into the property, if you separate.

In addition to the Cohabitation Agreement it may also be necessary for you to enter into the following:

1. A trust deed relating to the ownership of your property (see pages 23-6).

2. Wills may need to be prepared (see chapter 7).

3. An Enduring Power of Attorney may be required (see chapter 8).

If you wish to have complicated calculations to reflect the way in which you own a property, then it is a good idea to take legal advice in order to ensure that the agreement is clear. The precedent that we have included is a very simple one and is only meant to be a guide as to how to draft a Cohabitation Agreement rather than a definitive way of drafting one. If you want a more complicated agreement, therefore, you are advised to see a solicitor. **Remember, do not include any non-legal issues in this document**.

Reviews of the Cohabitation Agreement

As time goes on your relationship will change and significant things could happen in your life which may make the terms of the Cohabitation Agreement unfair and unjust and, as a result, unlikely to be upheld by the courts. If anything substantial happens in your relationship you should therefore consider re-drafting the Cohabitation Agreement. Such circumstances would include the following:

- The birth of a child.

- One of you becoming seriously ill.

- One of you becoming disabled.

- Redundancy.

- A significant change in your financial circumstances or the financial contributions you each make towards your relationship and your home.

- One of you receiving a large inheritance.

Again, the above list is not exhaustive and you should therefore consider entering into a new agreement in the event of any substantial change in your circumstances. Remember also that if you do decide to marry, the Cohabitation Agreement will not be binding upon the court or between you and, at best, it will simply provide evidence of what your intentions were towards each other when you were living together. If you wish to have an agreement, therefore, that may be treated as being binding between you in the event that you subsequently get married and your marriage breaks down, then you will need to enter into a Pre-nuptial Agreement; this can be very similar to a Cohabitation Agreement but it must state clearly that it is a Pre-nuptial Agreement. Legal advice should be taken before entering into such a document and again, it is not necessarily binding upon the courts or you.

Example Cohabitation Agreement

This Deed is made on *[INSERT DATE]* BETWEEN:–

1. **TONY ARTHUR SMITH** ('Tony') of 23 Chankly Bore, Zemmery Fidd, Dorset; and
2. **VALERIE MARY JUDD** ('Val') of 23 Chankly Bore, Zemmery Fidd, Dorset.

WHEREAS:–

1.
   a) We wish to enter in to an Agreement which regulates our rights and obligations to each other;
   b) We have taken independent legal advice;[1]
   c) We have disclosed to each other our respective financial positions (schedules of our respective income, assets and liabilities are attached);[2]
   d) We intend the terms of this Agreement to be legally binding;
   e) We are entering into this Agreement of our own free will and have not been put under any pressure to sign into it.

2. The terms of this Agreement:–
   a) are effective from the date written above;
   b) are severable;[3]
   c) are to be interpreted by the Courts of England and Wales which Courts we intend to have jurisdiction in relation to it.

3. *[INSERT ADDRESS OF PROPERTY HERE]*
   a) this is to be purchased/transferred into our joint names and held by us as tenants in common so that if either of us dies, that person's share will be dealt with in accordance with that person's Will/Law of Intestacy; or in the alternative
   b) is to be held by us as joint tenants so if either of us were to die, his/her share will pass automatically to the survivor regardless of any Will etc;[4]
   c) the purchase price of the property was [£   ] which we raised as follows:–
      i) £......... by way of mortgage from [   ] Building Society;
      ii) contribution towards the deposit from Tony of [£   ]
      iii) contribution towards the deposit from Val of [£   ]

---

[1] It is important for both parties to have received independent legal advice before they enter into an Agreement. Any Agreement is then less likely to be rejected by the Court.

[2] Don't forget to prepare these.

[3] So that if any part of the Agreement is declared invalid, the remaining clauses will remain valid.

[4] Refer to page 6 regarding the difference between joint tenants and tenants in common. It is important to delete which is inapplicable here.

(Continued on next page)

d) the following policies are linked to the mortgage and in the event of death of either of us the proceeds will be paid over to reduce the mortgage account:–

Name of insurance company	Policy No.	Life Assured	Death benefit	% in the policy owned by Tony	% in the policy owned by Val

    i) Tony will pay the premiums on the following policies:–
       [LIST]

    ii) Val will pay the premiums on the following policies:–
       [LIST]

    iii) We will jointly contribute towards the policies on the following percentage basis as follows:–
       [LIST]

THIS DEED evidences that we have agreed as follows:–
Shares in *[STATE FULL ADDRESS OF FAMILY HOME HERE]:–*

4.   a) Tony will own [   ] % of the property and Val will own the remaining [   ] %;[5]
    b) We will contribute towards any necessary repairs or improvements to *[ADDRESS OF PROPERTY]* in these proportions.[6]

5.   **Outgoings**
We will contribute towards the outgoings of the property in these proportions (or state otherwise if appropriate). These outgoings are as follows:–
   - Buildings insurance
   - Council tax
   - Service charges
   - (continue to list here)

6.   **Other outgoings on *[ADDRESS OF PROPERTY HERE]:–***
    i) Unless we agree something else in writing or a Court makes an Order which is different, we agree to make equal contributions towards all of the utilities on the property namely:–

---

[5] Different percentages are only applicable if a tenancy in common.

[6] If you keep to the same percentages for all contributions towards repairs, contributions towards mortgage payments and all outgoings which relate to the property (as opposed to outgoings that relate to the occupation of the property such as gas, electricity etc), then it will be much easier to calculate exactly what you both own at the end of the day.

(Continued on next page)

- Gas
- Electricity
- Water rates
- Telephone
- Oil

ii)   If either of us leaves the property permanently and the other remains in occupation, then:–

- We will continue to pay the outgoings listed above at 6(i) in the following percentage:
Tony   %
Val   %
for the period of three months following the separation date
- The one remaining in occupation will pay all of the aforementioned outgoings three months and one day after the date of separation until they permanently leave the property
- From the date of separation we will contribute to the mortgage instalments as follows: Tony [   ]% Val [   ]%
- In the event that one party does not meet their prescribed percentage of the mortgage instalments, then upon the sale of the property account will be taken of this so that the party who has paid more than their prescribed share of the mortgage instalments is fully compensated for this.

iii) After the date of our separation we will continue to pay the premiums on the policies in the shares prescribed above at paragraph 3(d) above.

7.   **Improvements**
We agree:–

a) to carry out any improvements, including repairs, which increase the value of [NAME OF PROPERTY] only by agreement between us or as recommended by a Chartered Surveyor appointed (and paid for) by us together (and if we cannot agree then as appointed by the President for the time being of the Royal Institute of Chartered Surveyors);

b) to pay for equally/in proportions in which we own [ADDRESS OF PROPERTY] the cost and work involved;

c) In the event that this is not done and neither of us pays a greater sum then upon the sale of the property or transfer of the property in accordance with the terms of this Deed the

(Continued on next page)

party who paid for the improvement shall be entitled to seek repayment and to charge interest at 3% interest per annum above Bank of England base rate on the sum paid

8.   **Sale or transfer of the property**

(i) Within the period of three months following the date of separation, one of us may offer to buy out the other's interest in it at an agreed price. In order to agree the price, three local estate agents will be asked to give valuations for the property but in the event that the value still cannot be agreed, then we will request the President of the Institute of Chartered Surveyors for the time being to nominate a local valuer to value the property and that valuation will become binding upon us and the sums due to us shall be calculated in accordance with that value. The cost of the valuation will be borne equally between us.

ii) In the event that an offer is made by one of us in accordance with paragraph 8(i) above, then all best endeavours must be made to ensure that the completion of the purchase of the other party's share is completed within six months of the date of separation.

9.   In the event that one of us does not purchase the other's share in the property, in accordance with paragraphs 8(i) and 8(ii) above, then we will market the property as agreed and in default of agreement we will:–

i)   invite immediately no less than one estate agent each to consider the marketing strategy to be employed to dispose of the property at the best price reasonably obtainable within the period of three months from the date of instruction;

ii) instruct each of the agents to report to us both simultaneously within one week in writing on the strategy they each recommend;

iii) market the property in accordance with the proposed strategies;

iv) require each of the respective agents to report to us simultaneously on each inspection arranged at the property and any offer made for the purchase of it;
v)   to market the property pending exchange of contracts;

vi) if we do not agree the firm of solicitors to use, we will use *[NAME FIRM OF SOLICITORS HERE]*

10.   **The net sale of proceeds of the property**

(Continued on next page)

From the gross sale proceeds of the sale of the property, we will pay:–

    i)   the estate agent's fees or other marketing expenses;
    ii) the legal costs of sale;
    iii) whatever is required to pay off the mortgage secured on the property.

The balance will be divided between us in the proportions set out at paragraph 4 above. In the event that the gross sale proceeds of the property are not enough to meet all of the above, then we will each pay one half of the shortfall at least 7 days prior to the completion of the sale to the solicitor having conduct of the conveyancing.

11.   **Dealing with the proceeds of the policies**

The policies which are held in our respective sole names shall be retained by the policyholders. The joint policies shall be divided between us in accordance with the contributions made by us towards the premiums and in the event that the said premiums are paid from our joint account, equally between us. We hereby agree to co-operate with each other in relation to the sale or surrender of the policies in order to achieve the best price achievable.

12.   **New home**

In the event that we sell *[STATE ADDRESS OF PROPERTY]* and purchase another property, we will enter into a new Agreement at the time of purchase, setting out our interest in that property.

13.   **Further promises about the property**

    i)   Neither of us will allow any other person into occupation of the property unless the period of 3 months referred to in paragraph 6(ii) above has expired and it is necessary, for the party remaining in occupation, to obtain financial assistance from another person in order to meet the mortgage payments and associated policy payments in full.
    ii) Neither of us will do anything which makes the building or contents insurance cover lapse or terminate.

14.   **Bank accounts**

We will maintain the following joint accounts:–

    i) *[LIST HERE]*

(Continued on next page)

    ii) We will make equal contributions to the aforesaid joint accounts on the first of each month until the first happens of:–

       a) a new agreement;

       b) either of us dying;

       c) three months after the separation date.

    iii) We will discharge all outgoings which relate to the occupation of the property from account number [   ][6]

    iv) We will make no unreasonable withdrawal from any of the joint accounts without the agreement of the other;

    v) We will co-operate with each other in relation to the closing of the aforesaid joint accounts immediately upon three months after the date of separation;

    vi) If either of us die, the other will become entitled to a credit balance on any of the joint accounts but may seek a one half contribution towards any debit balance from any other assets in the deceased's estate.

15.   **Things we will own in the future**

    i) Gifts (including inheritances) will belong to the person who receives them;

    ii) Any asset will be owned by the person who paid for it;

    iii) In the event that an asset is purchased out of the joint account, then it is to be owned equally and upon separation it shall be agreed which party shall retain the item and they will compensate the other by paying one half of the 'as new' price to the other;

    iv) In the event that a gift is made to both of us by friends or family of one of us, then the person whose family or friends gave the gift shall retain the item in the event of separation or death;

    v) In the event of our separation, then unless one of us can release the other from any joint hire purchase liability, then any item on hire purchase or similar will be sold and we will pay the proceeds towards the hire purchase account and take such steps as shall be required to discharge equally any remaining balance to include, if necessary, taking out a loan in our sole name.

---

[6] E.g. gas, electricity, water rates, telephone etc.

(Continued on next page)

16. **Personal items**

    We will each be entitled to remove from the property upon the separation date:–

    a) our personal possessions to include clothing, personal jewellery and things relating to our work (regardless of who paid for them);

    b) things we each owned prior to the dating of this Deed;

    c) gifts we have personally received (to include inheritances);

    d) things that Tony has purchased from …………..

    e) things that Val has purchased from ……………

17. The remainder of the contents shall be divided as though they are jointly owned, a coin will be tossed in front of an independent witness to determine who shall retain the item and which party shall pay the relevant proportion of the new value to the person who loses the item.

    We have signed this document and had it witnessed because we intend it to be a Deed and be binding upon us:–

Signed by **TONY ARTHUR SMITH**   …………………………………..

In the presence of

…………………….................................. (witness signature)

Witness name……………………………….

Witness address …………………………….

………………………………………………..

………………………………………………..

Witness occupation …………………………

Signed by **VALERIE MARY JUDD**   …………………………………..

In the presence of

…………………….................................. (witness signature)

Witness name……………………………….

Witness address …………………………….

………………………………………………..

………………………………………………..

Witness occupation …………………………

Children

4

The law relating to children is governed by the Children Act 1989. This Act lays down the general principle of child law which is that:

When any court determines any question with respect to:

(a) the upbringing of the child; or

(b) the administration of the child's property or the application of any income arising from it;

the child's welfare shall be the court's 'paramount consideration'.

Accordingly, the child's welfare is the court's sole concern whenever it is asked to consider any issues in relation to the child and any other factors are only relevant to the extent that they assist the court in determining the best solution for that child. This chapter sets out the types of order that a court can make in relation to a child on an application by either parent. They are:

- Parental responsibility orders
- Residence orders
- Contact orders
- Prohibited steps orders
- Specific issue orders

Lastly, the chapter covers child abduction (the subject of applications by one parent against another for financial assistance with children, in the event of separation, is discussed in chapter 9).

The Children Act makes it clear that the court should not make any order unless it is necessary. This is known as the principle of 'no order'. In practical terms, this means that if the parents agree how a child should be brought up and all other arrangements for its welfare, the court will not intervene unless necessary. As a child gets older and becomes more able to make their own decisions, the court will take more notice of the child's views on an issue. The age at which a child can make a reasoned decision obviously differs with each child but generally, the court will consider a child's views from the age of 9 and begin to take them more seriously from around the age of 12. In relation to medical intervention, the case of Gillick established that children who are under 16 may obtain medical assistance without the consent of their parents providing it can be shown that they are of sufficient age and understanding. In any event, any child over the age of 16 can obtain medical treatment without the consent from a parent or guardian.

Parental responsibility

If parents are married they each have equal parental responsibility for their children (but not for stepchildren) which cannot be lost on divorce. If parents are not married the natural mother has sole parental responsibility for the children and the father has none, unless the parents have entered into a Parental Responsibility Agreement (see chapter 5 for full details) or a court has made an order giving parental responsibility to the father.

Parental responsibility gives the parents all of the 'rights, duties, powers, responsibilities and authority which by law a parent has in relation to a child and his property'. Its practical effect is that where two parents have parental responsibility, one parent cannot make unilateral decisions about the child without the other agreeing the matter with them first. If this is not possible, then one of the parents must apply to the court for the court to decide the issue. The types of issue that are covered by parental responsibility are such things as the child's education, religious instruction and medical care.

Residence

Residence is the legal term which replaces the old concept of custody and is the type of order that a court will make when it is necessary for the court to decide where a child should live. A residence order can be made in favour of one parent or on rare occasions, in favour of both parents, but usually only when they share the care of the children. Where parents agree where the children should have their main base, no residence order is required at all.

Contact

Contact is the legal term that replaces the old concept of 'access'. It is used to refer to the time that the parent who does not have the day-to-day care of the children can see them. Usually, parents agree the arrangements for contact between them, but if they cannot, a court may make an order for contact. Contact can include overnight (also known as 'staying') contact or supervised contact where it is thought that the child should not be left alone with their parent.

Certain third parties, e.g. grandparents and step-parents, can also apply for contact with a child although they have to ask the permission of the court in the first instance (such permission is usually granted).

Prohibited steps orders

These can be applied for if it is necessary to obtain an order to prevent something happening in relation to a child, e.g. to prevent them having contact with an undesirable person or to stop a parent from taking them to a particular place.

Specific issue orders

These are the orders a court will make for any other issue relating to a child which is not covered by residence, contact or prohibited steps orders. They are usually orders made by a court when it is asked to make a decision about an important aspect of the child's life, e.g. whether it should emigrate with a parent, or what school it should attend.

Child abduction

Under the Child Abduction Act 1984, it is a criminal offence for a parent to remove or send a child from the country where he or she usually lives without the other parent's permission providing *only* that the other parent has parental responsibility under the laws of that country. If you want to move to another country, therefore, (and this includes if you are living in Scotland and moving the child to England or Wales, or vice versa) then you must agree this with the parent with parental responsibility, or alternatively make an application to the court. This means that a natural mother, where the father does not have parental responsibility, may therefore remove or send a child to where they wish and not be guilty of the crime of abduction. Furthermore, a father without parental responsibility *cannot* take the child out of the jurisdiction without the mother's agreement or leave of the court.

If you are unable to agree on an issue with your partner about your children, then it is particularly important to try to avoid an application to the court if at all possible. Court applications should be treated as a last resort. Mediation can provide a more appropriate forum for negotiating arrangements for children in a safe environment. Other sources of help can include a family therapist, the guidance service 'Relate' or a counsellor.

Parental responsibility

5

A Parental Responsibility Agreement is a legal document signed by both parents of a child, when they are unmarried. The Agreement gives parental responsibility to the mother (who naturally has parental responsibility from birth), as well as to the father.

If the parents cannot agree to enter into a Parental Responsibility Agreement then the parent without parental responsibility (i.e. the father) must obtain an order from the court. If a non-parent obtains a residence order from the court (for details of residence see chapter 4, 'Children') the residence order will automatically carry with it parental responsibility.

Parental responsibility gives the father of a child the same rights, duties, powers, responsibilities and authority for the child as the mother has. A Parental Responsibility Agreement lasts until the child's 18th birthday, or until revoked by order of the court. A court will only revoke the Agreement, however, if the child or one of the parents applies for it to be revoked.

Signing a Parental Responsibility Agreement

A Parental Responsibility Agreement can only be signed by the natural (i.e. biological) parents of the child. Step-parents, grand-parents, adoptive parents or any other relation of the child should not sign a Parental Responsibility Agreement. If they wish to obtain parental responsibility, then they must apply to the Court for an Order.

Obtaining a Parental Responsibility Agreement

In order to obtain parental responsibility, the parents have to both sign the Agreement and attend court together to lodge the same. The following needs to be brought to the court by the parents, as proof of identification:

Preferred evidence:

- Passport
- Photo card
- Student card

Acceptable evidence:

- Income Support book
- Child Benefit book
- Driver's licence
- Sports/membership cards (preferably with a photograph)
- Work/security passes (preferably with a photograph)
- Banker's card
- Firearm's licence
- Prison number

Acceptable in specific circumstances:

- When the parents have been identified in a court case concerning the child, there is no need for them to produce further identification, as long as there is a covering letter explaining the circumstances and at what court the hearing was held and the case number.

When a Parental Responsibility Agreement is taken to court, the clerk who deals with the matter must check the Agreement for the child's surname. If it differs from the name of both parents then this will be queried and proof must be given as to why the child has been given this surname.

The Agreement form must be fully completed. Any 'care of' address must be explained and solicitors' addresses will not be accepted.

After the check has been made by the clerk of the court, the clerk will ask to see identity as listed above. If no evidence is produced then the Agreement cannot be witnessed.

Parents can only sign the Agreement in the presence of the court clerk who witnesses it. The Clerk has to check that they are the natural parents and will complete the certificate of witness and sign and date the Agreement, entering the address and court stamp. After doing this, the Clerk will return the Agreement to the parents for them to send to the Principal Registry where it will be registered.

It is possible for parents to attend any county court to sign a Parental Responsibility Agreement, but it will only actually be registered at the Principal Registry.

If you have any further queries about Parental Responsibility Agreements you are advised to contact the Children Section of the Principal Registry of the Family Division (see Appendix 2).

Parental Responsibility Agreement
Section 4(1)(b) Children Act 1989

Read the notes before you make this agreement.

Keep this form in a safe place
Date recorded at the Principal Registry of the Family Division

This is a Parental Responsibility Agreement regarding

the Child
Name

Boy or Girl   *Date of birth*   *Date of 18th birthday*

Between
the Mother
Name

Address

and
the Father
Name

Address

We declare that
we are the mother and father of the above child and we agree that the child's father shall have parental responsibility for the child (in addition to the mother having parental responsibility).

Signed (**Mother**)

Signed (**Father**)

Date

Date

Certificate of witness

The following evidence of identity was produced by the person signing above:

The following evidence of identity was produced by the person signing above:

Signed in the presence of:
Name of Witness

Signed in the presence of:
Name of Witness

Address

Address

Signature of Witness

Signature of Witness

[A Justice of the Peace] [Justice's Clerk]
[An Officer of the Court authorised by the judge to administer oaths]

[A Justice of the Peace] [Justice's Clerk]
[An Officer of the Court authorised by the judge to administer oaths]

C(PRA)-w3 (9.99)

Reproduced by Law Pack Publishing with the permission of the Controller of HMSO

(Continued on next page)

Parental Responsibility Agreement (continued)

Notes about the Parental Responsibility Agreement

Read these notes before you make the agreement.

About the Parental Responsibility Agreement

The making of this agreement will affect the legal position of the mother and the father. You should both seek legal advice before you make the Agreement. You can obtain the name and address of a solicitor from the Children Panel (020 7242 1222) or from

- your local proceedings court, or county court
- a Citizens Advice Bureau
- a Law Centre
- a local library.

You may be eligible for legal aid.

When you fill in the Agreement

Please use black ink (the Agreement will be copied). Put the name of one child only. If the father is to have parental responsibility for more than one child, fill in a separate form for each child. **Do not sign the Agreement.**

When you have filled in the Agreement

Take it to a local family proceedings court, or county court, or the Principal Registry of the Family Division (the address is below).

A justice of the peace, a justice's clerk, or a court official who is authorised by the judge to administer oaths, will witness your signature and he or she will sign the certificate of the witness.

To the mother: When you make the declaration you will have to prove that you are the child's mother so take to the court the child's full birth certificate.
You will also need evidence of your identity showing a photograph and signature (for example, a photocard, official pass or passport).

To the father: You will need evidence of your identity showing a photograph and signature (for example, a photocard, official pass or passport).

When the Certificate has been signed and witnessed

Make 2 copies of the of form. You do not need to copy these notes.
Take, or send, this form and the copies to The Principal Registry of the Family Division, First Avenue House, 42–49 High Holbom, London, WC 1V 6NP.

The Registry will record the Agreement and keep this form. The copies will be stamped and sent back to each parent at the address on the Agreement. The Agreement will not take effect until it has been received and recorded at the Principal Registry of the Family Division.

Ending the Agreement

Once a parental responsibility agreement has been made it can only end
- by an order of the court made on the application of any person who has parental responsibility for the child
- by an order of the court made on the application of the child with leave of the court
- when the child reaches the age of 18

C(PRA)-(Notes)

Domestic violence

6

Non-molestation injunction

The law providing protection against molestation is now the same for unmarried couples who live together and for married couples. Under the Family Law Act 1996, both are entitled to non-molestation orders, providing they come within the definition of the term 'associated'. Under the Act, a person is associated with another if they:

i)   are married;

ii) are cohabitants or former cohabitants;

iii) have lived in the same house, other than merely by reason of one of them being the other's employee, tenant, lodger or boarder;

iv) are relatives;

v)   have agreed to marry one another (whether or not that agreement has been terminated);

vi) in relation to any child, are either a parent of that child or have or have had parental responsibility for the child; or

vii) are parties to the same family proceedings (other than the non-molestation proceedings).

Note that the term 'cohabitant' relates only to men and women who live together, *not* to homosexual couples. Homosexual couples who live together, however, are still associated because of the definition at (iii) above. If they do not or have not lived together then they are not 'associated' and they must apply for protection under the Protection from Harassment Act (see below).

The definition of molestation is quite wide and does not involve just violence. Reported cases show that molestation includes harassment and threats of violence. Molestation would therefore include such things as following somebody, telephoning them repeatedly, sending notes through their door, etc. If anyone with whom you are 'associated' has done any of these things, you therefore could be entitled to a non-molestation injunction.

Occupation orders

When it comes to excluding one person from the family home, the law is different for people who are unmarried and who live together, and those who are or have been married. We will not trouble ourselves with the law as it relates to married people in this Guide and will turn straight to the law as it relates to cohabitants.

If the person applying for the occupation order (the applicant) has either a legal or a beneficial interest in the property, i.e. through ownership or tenancy (see chapter 2 for a definition of beneficial interest), then they may find it relatively easy to obtain an occupation order against their cohabitant or former cohabitant. If, however, the applicant does not have a legal or beneficial interest in the property, i.e. through ownership or a tenancy agreement, then they can only apply for an occupation order against the person they have been living with providing they are or have been in a heterosexual cohabiting relationship.

When deciding whether to make an occupation order, the court will consider whether the order should be to exclude completely the person against whom the application is made (the respondent) from the property or just from a particular area of the property (e.g. an office or a bedroom) or from an area surrounding the property.

The court will take into account the following factors:

a) The housing needs and resources of each of the parties and of any relevant child.

Therefore, if one party is asking for an occupation order excluding their cohabitant or former cohabitant from the property and it is clear to the court that if they do this one party is going to end up homeless, the court may not make the order that the applicant seeks.

b) The financial resources of each of the parties.

If the applicant is much wealthier than the responding party, it may be that the applicant will not be successful.

c) The likely effect of any order or any decision *not* to exercise its powers on health, safety or well-being of the parties and of any relevant child (medical reports, etc., might be useful evidence here).

So if the making of the order will be particularly beneficial to one party or a child, the court is more likely to make the order.

d) The conduct of the parties in relation to each other.

If the responding party has not behaved badly towards the applicant, the applicant may not be successful.

When making any occupation order between cohabitants, the court has to consider the nature of the parties' relationship and it is asked by the Act to have regard to the fact that 'they have not given each other the commitment involved in marriage'. In practical terms this means that if the cohabiting relationship was not of long duration and did not involve a lot of commitment, then the applicant is less likely to be successful in obtaining an occupation order.

In certain instances, if it appears to the court that the harm that will be suffered by the respondent or any child, in the event that an occupation order is made, is going to be greater than the harm that would be suffered by the applicant if the order is not made, then the court will not make the order.

When making an occupation order, the court may make orders relating to the following:

- obligations as to the repair and maintenance of the family home;

- the discharge of bank, mortgage repayments or other outgoings affecting the family home;

- the payment of 'occupational rent' by the party in occupation of the family home or any part of it to the other party;

- granting either party possession or use of furniture or other contents of the family home;

- provision that either party take reasonable care of any furniture or other contents of the dwelling house;

- provision that either party takes steps to keep the family home or any furniture or other contents secure.

When deciding what orders to make of this nature, the court will have regard to all the circumstances, including the financial needs, resources and obligations that the parties have or are likely to have in the future, including any financial obligations they may have towards each other or to any relevant child (i.e. whether they can afford such an order).

The prescribed court form for applying for a non-molestation and occupation order can be found at the Court Service website (see Appendix 1). You are advised to take legal advice before bringing such an application; court staff are usually extremely helpful.

Protection from Harassment Act

If you are being harassed by somebody and they do not come within the definition of 'associated' above and you thus cannot obtain a non-molestation injunction against them under the Family Law Act 1996 (e.g. because you are a homosexual couple who never lived together), then you may be able to bring an application for an injunction under the Protection from Harassment Act 1996. These injunctions can be brought both on a civil basis (i.e. by making your own application to your local county court), or on a criminal basis, which would involve your going to your local police and asking them to bring the proceedings for you.

Wills and what happens if you die without one

7

The law in relation to cohabitants in the event of one of them predeceasing the other is very different to the law relating to married couples. If you are a married couple and one person leaves a Will under which they exclude the other spouse or leave an inadequate amount of money, then that spouse can make an application under the Inheritance (Provision for Family and Dependants) Act 1975, under which they will ask the court to adjust the Will so that they receive sufficient monies from the estate of the deceased.

If a married person dies without a Will then the law of intestacy will apply under which their spouse will automatically receive a large part of their estate (see details of the law of intestacy below).

If you are living with someone unmarried, and they die and they do not leave a Will, or they do not leave you sufficient monies under their Will, then you can only apply under the Inheritance (Provision for Family and Dependants) Act for monies out of their estate in relatively limited circumstances, which are:

- that you were financially dependent upon the deceased at the time of death; and/or

- you had been living with the deceased for a continuous period of at least two years immediately prior to the date of death.

It is obviously of help in these circumstances that you have good evidence as to what you had agreed should happen in the event of death and for this reason it is a good idea to refer to the provision you intend to make for each other in your Wills in your Cohabitation Agreement. A Cohabitation Agreement alone, however, is not sufficient since there are very strict rules about how Wills are drawn up and executed.

The law of intestacy makes no provision at all for somebody who cohabits. The law of intestacy says that if there is no Will then the estate is divided as follows:

1. The total estate goes to a surviving spouse where there are no children, parents, brothers or sisters.

2. If the deceased is survived by a spouse and children, the spouse will get the chattels (i.e. personal possessions) and a fixed sum (currently £125,000). In addition, the spouse will have the right to use one half of the remaining estate for the rest of their life and on their death it will then pass to the deceased's children. The remaining half-share goes directly to any children.

3. If there is a surviving spouse and a parent or brothers and sisters but no children, it is the same as for no. 2 above but the fixed sum received by the surviving spouse is increased to £200,000.

4. The total estate passes to the issue of the deceased if there is no surviving spouse.

5. If there is no surviving spouse or children, then the estate passes to the blood relatives of the deceased in order of closeness, starting with his parents.

If the party who died was not married, therefore, their estate will *not* automatically pass to the person they were living with, however long that relationship may have lasted.

It is therefore particularly important that people who live together make Wills. If they do not, under the law of intestacy, the surviving partner may receive no monies at all and will have to try and establish a claim under the Inheritance (Provision for Family and Dependants Act) 1975. If they have not been financially dependent and were not living with the deceased for two years immediately prior to their death (e.g. because the deceased was in a nursing home) then they may have nothing at all. In such circumstances, the law can be very unfair towards cohabitants.

Law Pack's Last Will & Testament Guide gives full details of how to make a Will and discusses the issues to bear in mind. An example Will is provided but you are recommended to take legal advice upon this and to read the Law Pack Guide.

When you make a Will, it is important that you bear in mind the following:

1. The person who makes the Will must be free to dispose of his estate as he wants.

2. The person who makes the Will must have had the mental capacity to do so and must not have been under any undue influence by another person to make it, or the Will can be invalidated.

3. It must be signed by the testator (i.e. person making the Will) at the foot.

4. It must be dated.

5. The signature must be witnessed by two people (as to who those people should be, see below).

6. They must witness each other's signature.

7. The testator must also witness their signatures, i.e. they should all be present.

The usual clause at the end of the Will creates the presumption that this has been complied with.

It is for this reason that a Cohabitation Agreement can never be treated as though it were a Will and it is a good idea to execute a Will at the same time as you enter into your Cohabitation Agreement.

Any person who witnesses a Will disentitles himself and their spouse from receiving any gift under the Will. Accordingly, if you wish to leave a legacy to someone, that person must **not** be a witness to your Will.

Example Last Will & Testament

Last Will & Testament

PRINT NAME AND ADDRESS

THIS Last Will & Testament is made by me *GILLIAN ROSS*
of *5 MAPLE TERRACE, LONDON SW10 2PZ*

I REVOKE all previous wills and codicils.

EXECUTORS' NAMES AND ADDRESSES

I APPOINT as executors and trustees of my will

DAVID PETER ROSS and *THERESA ANN MUNDY*
of *5 MAPLE TERRACE* of *9 KING'S WALK*
LONDON SW10 2PZ *LEAMINGTON SPA LM9 2BL*

SUBSTITUTIONAL EXECUTOR'S NAME AND ADDRESS

and should one or more of them fail to or be unable to act I APPOINT to fill any vacancy

Anthony John Williams
of *17 St George's Crescent, Reading RG7 9XY*

SPECIFIC GIFTS AND LEGACIES

I GIVE *one thousand pounds to my friend Anthony John Williams*
my pearl stud earrings to my sister Ruth Elizabeth Jones of 11 The Groves,
Aberdeen AB3 4AZ
my gold locket to my sister Theresa Ann Mundy

Any legacy to a minor may be validly handed over to his/her parent or guardian.

RESIDUARY GIFT

I GIVE the residue of my estate to *David Peter Ross, Theresa Ann Mundy and*
Ruth Elizabeth Jones in equal shares

but if he/she or (if I have indicated more than one person) any of them fails to survive me by 28 days or if this gift or any part of it fails for any other reason, then I GIVE the residue of my estate or the part of it affected to
the other residuary beneficiaries in proportion to their shares

FUNERAL WISHES

I WISH my body to be ☑ buried ☐ cremated other instructions *in family grave at*
St. Catherine's Cemetery, London

DATE

SIGNED by the above-named testator in our presence on the *10th* day of *June* 20*00* and then by us in the testator's presence

TESTATOR'S SIGNATURE

SIGNED *Gillian Ross*

WITNESSES' SIGNATURES NAMES AND ADDRESSES

SIGNED *JP Smith* SIGNED *Susan Smith*
JOHN PETER SMITH *SUSAN JANE SMITH*
of *23 DEVONSHIRE ROAD,* of *23 DEVONSHIRE ROAD,*
OXFORD *OXFORD*
occupation *PLUMBER* occupation *HOUSEWIFE*

The person who makes the Will must have 'the requisite mental capacity'. This means: soundness of mind, memory and understanding, which means that they must understand:

- the nature of his acts and their broad effects;

- the extent of his property (although not necessarily every individual item); and

- the moral claims that they ought to consider (even if he decides to reject such claims and dispose of his property to other beneficiaries).

A Will is not sacrosanct and can always be attacked by any valid claim under the Inheritance (Provision for Family and Dependants) Act. Not only can cohabitants make a claim under this Act; spouses, ex-spouses and children can, too. When making a Will, therefore, you must bear in mind the claims that any 'first family' or any other relatives may have against your estate. There is no point in making a Will that will be challenged in court upon your death and that will then lead to costly, lengthy legal battles over your estate. This is the worst legacy that anybody can leave behind for their loved ones; it is therefore extremely important that you take legal advice upon any claims that your loved ones may have upon your estate, so that you have adequately dealt with them all in your Will so avoiding any future claims under the Inheritance Act. If you want to leave a close relative or dependant out of your Will, then it is a good idea to leave a note with your Will explaining why, since this will then provide good evidence for a court in the event that he makes a claim under the 1975 Act against your estate. See chapter 9 on making an application under the Inheritance (Provision for Family and Dependants) Act 1975 if (unhappily) you are in the position of having to make such a claim.

After death, a Will must be admitted to probate. It is then lodged at court and a copy issued in a folder which forms the grant of probate, which is an important document of title. Once that grant is six months old it can be very difficult to mount a claim under the Inheritance Act, so if you are to make such a claim, you must move very quickly after death. Again, see chapter 9.

Illness, incapacitation and death

8

Enduring Powers of Attorney ━━━━━

There is always the possibility that either you or your partner may become mentally incapable as a result of illness or accident. If you are married, it is unlikely that anybody would question a spouse dealing with the affairs of their wife/husband. However, if you are not married your partner will not automatically be viewed as your representative and it is therefore wise in these circumstances to draw up a formal document known as an Enduring Power of Attorney to authorise your partner to act on your behalf should you become mentally incapable.

Take care, however, because under the Enduring Powers of Attorney Act 1985 the person that you appoint under the Power of Attorney to act on your behalf cannot be removed by you if you become dissatisfied with the way in which they are acting on your behalf. You may therefore wish to restrict the authority of the Power of Attorney that you give but if you do so, this might mean that the Court of Protection has to be appointed to deal with any outstanding matters.

It is therefore absolutely vital that you trust the person to whom you give an Enduring Power of Attorney and if you are worried in any way about this, you probably should not do it.

The way in which it works

In this section 'the donor' means the person giving the Power of Attorney and the attorney is the person who is appointed to look after the donor's affairs. The power to act on the donor's behalf is given to 'the attorney' by the Enduring Power of Attorney document (see precedent attached). It is executed by the donor and by the other person 'the attorney' and is witnessed by an independent witness. The document must be prepared whilst the donor is mentally capable. Normally, the attorney has *immediate* authority to do all acts under the document unless a restriction is put in to prevent the attorney from doing any acts at all until the donor does become mentally incapable.

Until the donor becomes mentally incapable, they are able to withdraw the Enduring Power of Attorney at any time and to end it completely. All they have to do is give notice to the attorney and the attorney then becomes personally liable if he carries on regardless.

Mental incapacity means that an individual is incapable by reason of mental disorder of managing and administering their property and affairs. Once the donor does become incapable, the attorney has to apply for registration of the Enduring Power of Attorney and until this document has been registered, the attorney's powers are restricted to:

i)   taking action to maintain the donor and/or to prevent loss to his estate; and

ii) taking action to maintain himself or other persons that the donor might have been expected to maintain.

If at any time the attorney becomes bankrupt, then he can no longer act. Furthermore, the attorney can refuse or renounce the appointment simply by telling the donor that they do not want to do it/continue to do it providing the donor is still mentally capable. If the donor has become mentally incapable, however, the attorney can only refuse or renounce the appointment if he notifies the court who is then likely to appoint a Receiver under the Court of Protection Rules. Legal advice should be taken if you find yourself in this position.

If there are difficult matters for the attorney to decide (e.g. whether to sell or let a property), he can always approach the court for guidance to protect himself from personal liability. The court has a general power to impose conditions such as, for example, the filing of accounts every year by the attorney.

Example completed Enduring Power of Attorney

ENDURING POWER OF ATTORNEY

Part A: About using this form

1. **You may choose one attorney or more than one.** If you choose one attorney then you must delete everything between the square brackets on the first page of the form. If you choose more than one, you must decide whether they are able to act:
   - Jointly (that is, they must all act together and cannot act separately) or
   - Jointly and severally (that is, they can all act together but they can also act separately if they wish).

   On the first page of the form, show what you have decided by crossing out one of the alternatives.

2. **If you give your attorney(s) general power** in relation to all your property and affairs, it means that they will be able to deal with your money or property and may be able to sell your house.

3. **If you don't want your attorney(s) to have such wide powers**, you can include any restrictions you like. For example, you can include a restriction that your attorney(s) must not act on your behalf until they have reason to believe that you are becoming mentally incapable; or a restriction as to what your attorney(s) may do. Any restrictions you choose must be written or typed where indicated on the second page of the form.

4. **If you are a trustee** (and please remember that co-ownership of a home involves trusteeship), you should seek legal advice if you want your attorney(s) to act as a trustee on your behalf.

5. **Unless you put in a restriction preventing it** your attorney(s) will be able to use any of your money or property to make any provision which you yourself might be expected to make for their own needs or the needs of other people. Your attorney(s) will also be able to use your money to make gifts, but only for reasonable amounts in relation to the value of your money and property.

6. **Your attorney(s) can recover the out-of-pocket expenses** of acting as your attorney(s). If your attorney(s) are professional people, for example solicitors or accountants, they may be able to charge for their professional services as well. You may wish to provide expressly for remuneration of your attorney(s) (although if they are trustees they may not be allowed to accept it).

7. **If your attorney(s) have reason to believe that** you have become or are becoming mentally incapable of managing your affairs, your attorney(s) will have to apply to the Court of Protection for registration of this power.

8. **Before applying to the Court of Protection for registration** of this power, your attorney(s) must give written notice that that is what they are going to do, to you and your nearest relatives as defined in the Enduring Powers of Attorney Act 1985. You or your relatives will be able to object if you or they disagree with registration.

9. **This is a simplified explanation** of what the Enduring Powers of Attorney Act 1985 and the Rules and Regulations say. If you need more guidance, you or your advisers will need to look at the Act itself and the Rules and Regulations. The Rules are the Court of Protection (Enduring Powers of Attorney) Rules 1986 (Statutory Instrument 1986 No. 127). The Regulations are the Enduring Powers of Attorney (Prescribed Form) Regulations 1990 (Statutory Instrument 1990 No. 1376).

10. **Note to Attorney(s)**
    After the power has been registered you should notify the Court of Protection if the donor dies or recovers.

11. **Note to Donor**
    Some of these explanatory notes may not apply to the form you are using if it has already been adapted to suit your particular requirements.

YOU CAN CANCEL THIS POWER AT ANY TIME BEFORE IT HAS TO BE REGISTERED

(Continued on next page)

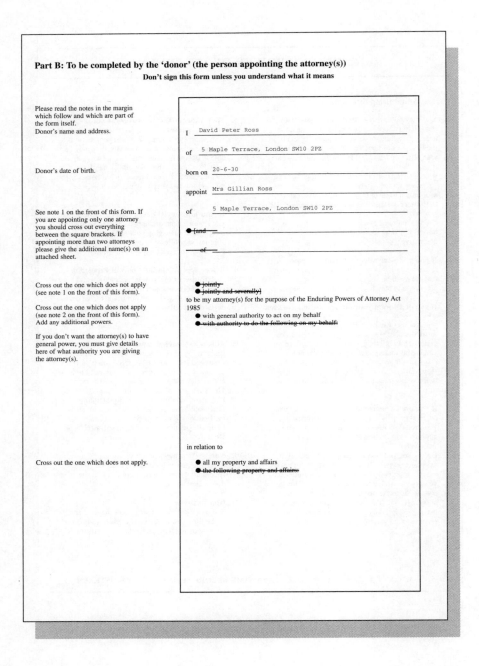

Part B: To be completed by the 'donor' (the person appointing the attorney(s))

Don't sign this form unless you understand what it means

Please read the notes in the margin which follow and which are part of the form itself.
Donor's name and address.

I   David Peter Ross

of   5 Maple Terrace, London SW10 2PZ

Donor's date of birth.

born on   20-6-30

appoint   Mrs Gillian Ross

See note 1 on the front of this form. If you are appointing only one attorney you should cross out everything between the square brackets. If appointing more than two attorneys please give the additional name(s) on an attached sheet.

of   5 Maple Terrace, London SW10 2PZ

● [and ——

—— of ——

Cross out the one which does not apply (see note 1 on the front of this form).

● jointly
● jointly and severally]

Cross out the one which does not apply (see note 2 on the front of this form). Add any additional powers.

to be my attorney(s) for the purpose of the Enduring Powers of Attorney Act 1985
    ● with general authority to act on my behalf
    ● with authority to do the following on my behalf:

If you don't want the attorney(s) to have general power, you must give details here of what authority you are giving the attorney(s).

in relation to

Cross out the one which does not apply.

    ● all my property and affairs
    ● the following property and affairs:

(Continued on next page)

Example completed Enduring Power of Attorney *(continued)*

Part B: continued

Please read the notes in the margin which follow and which are part of the form itself.
If there are restrictions or conditions, insert them here; if not, cross out these words if you wish (see note 3 on the front of this form).

~~● subject to the following restrictions and conditions:~~

If this form is being signed at your direction: —
● the person signing must not be an attorney or any witness (to Parts B or C);
● you must add a statement that this form has been signed at your direction;
● a second witness is necessary (please see below).

I intend that this power shall continue even if I become mentally incapable.

I have read or have had read to me the notes in Part A which are part of, and explain, this form.

Your signature (or mark).

Signed by me as a deed and delivered   *David P. Ross*

Date.

on   10th April 2001

Someone must witness your signature.

Signature of witness.

in the presence of   *Thomas Waite*

Your attorney(s) cannot be your witness. It is not advisable for your husband or wife to be your witness.

Full name of witness   Thomas Waite

Address of witness   36 Amber Road

London SW3 5HM

A second witness is only necessary if this form is not being signed by you personally but at your direction (for example, if a physical disability prevents you from signing).

Signature of second witness.

in the presence of

Full name of witness

Address of witness

(Continued on next page)

Part C: To be completed by the attorney(s)

Note 1. This form may be adapted to provide for execution by a corporation.

2. If there is more than one attorney additional sheets in the form as shown below must be added to this Part C.

Please read the notes in the margin which follow and which are part of the form itself.

Don't sign this form before the donor has signed Part B or if, in your opinion, the donor was already mentally incapable at the time of signing Part B.

If this form is being signed at your direction: —

- the person signing must not be an attorney or any witness (to Parts B or C);
- you must add a statement that this form has been signed at your direction;
- a second witness is necessary (please see below).

Signature (or mark) of attorney.

Date.

Signature of witness.

The attorney must sign the form and his signature must be witnessed. The donor may not be the witness and one attorney may not witness the signature of the other.

A second witness is only necessary if this form is not being signed by you personally but at your direction (for example, if a physical disability prevents you from signing).
Signature of second witness.

I understand that I have a duty to apply to the Court for the registration of this form under the Enduring Powers of Attorney Act 1985 when the donor is becoming or has become mentally incapable.

I also understand my limited power to use the donor's property to benefit persons other than the donor.

I am not a minor

Signed by me as a deed and delivered   *Gillian Ross*

on ___10th April 2001___

in the presence of   *Thomas Waite*

Full name of witness   Thomas Waite

Address of witness   36 Amber Road

London SW3 5HM

---

in the presence of _____

Full name of witness _____

Address of witness _____

Reproduced by Law Pack Publishing Ltd with the permission of the Controller of HMSO

The authority of the attorney

The attorney must bear in mind the following:

1. There are certain matters that an attorney can never do because of the law such as, for example, executing a Will on behalf of the donor.

2. The attorney has a duty to use the same care and skill as he would use in relation to the management of their own affairs. An attorney who fails in this duty could be liable in negligence if the donor suffers loss as a result.

3. The attorney will be personally liable for what he has done if the attorney does not have authority to act.

4. The law is generally wary about allowing attorneys to act in matters in which they have an interest (i.e. where they may benefit themselves). However, in certain circumstances the attorney may act so as to benefit himself or persons other than the donor to the following extent (and no further):

   - the attorney may act in relation to himself or in relation to any other person if the donor might be expected to provide for the attorney or the other person's needs – this would be particularly helpful if the attorney was the donor's partner and other people were the donor's and the attorney's children. Furthermore, the attorney may do whatever the donor might be expected to have done to meet those needs. **This may be very important for cohabitants since it *would* mean for example the attorney could pay family bills out of the donor's money.**

The attorney may dispose of the donor's property by way of gift to the following extent but no further:

   - the attorney may make gifts of a seasonal nature (e.g. birthday and Christmas presents to persons who are related or connected to the donor); and

   - the attorney may make gifts to any charity to whom the donor may or might be expected to make gifts.

However, the value of the gifts should be reasonable with respect to all the circumstances and in particular the size of the donor's estate. The attorney should not therefore make any sizeable transfers or gifts out of the donor's estate, either to himself or to others.

5. The attorney has no duty to do anything at all if he does not wish to, except they must always give notice (see below) and apply for registration in the event that the donor becomes mentally incapable.

Duties of the attorney

As soon as the attorney has reason to believe that the donor is or is becoming mentally incapable (and this may not mean that the donor actually is incapable!) he must act as follows:

1. He must notify any other attorney who has been appointed.

2. He must tell the donor that he will make an application for registration for the enduring power of attorney.

3. All of the people in the following groups must also be notified by completing and sending a specified document by first class post in the order in which they appear, until at least three people (counting the attorney if they are one of these people) are notified:

   i) the donor's spouse;

   ii) the donor's children;

   iii) the donor's parents;

   iv) the donor's brothers or sisters;

   v) a widow or widower of the donor's children;

   vi) any of the donor's grandchildren over the age of 18; and

   vii) the donor's nieces and nephews.

   These relatives can then object to the appointment if they wish.

There are further classes and specific legal advice should be obtained upon this if it is likely that these classes will be necessary.

The individuals listed above need not be notified if:

i)   their address is not known;

ii)   they are not over 18;

iii) they are mentally incapable; or

iv)   if the court gives permission or 'leave'.

4. Within three days after notice has been given, the attorney must lodge with the court:

    a) a specified document confirming compliance with the notice provisions;

    b) the original power;

    c) a fee (at the moment £30).

At that point, the attorney resumes full powers.

5. These are called the protection provisions because the court may refuse to allow registration of the Enduring Power of Attorney or it may respond to an objection given by the relatives listed above, because, in effect, this is a warning that there may be difficulties. The relatives have five weeks in which to object.

Refer to the Law Pack 'Powers of Attorney & Living Wills' for further details. An example of a completed Enduring Power of Attorney is provided on the pages 61-4.

The meaning of 'next of kin' and 'hospital proxies'

It is not clear under the law whether a cohabitant is next of kin to their partner when it comes to giving instructions regarding their partner's medical treatment. The position is made more complex when there are other family members competing for the role of next of kin or representative, such as a 'first family' (i.e. children by a first marriage).

Fortunately, there is a principle known as 'the doctrine of necessity' which justifies medical intervention; for example, in an emergency where an individual is not capable of giving a valid consent. As a result of this doctrine, cohabitants are often treated in the same way as a married couple by the medical profession. However, a cohabitant can still encounter difficulties with the medical profession if their partner is ill, particularly if their relationship has been one of short duration.

It is possible to provide a hospital with written documents declaring which person is to be your next of kin. It has no binding status; but it can be used as evidence if there is any dispute as to whom is to have this authority.

Most hospitals will provide a health care proxy appointment form which is more specific than a general next of kin appointment for a patient to execute. In it you give specific details of exactly what medical decisions can be taken as the proxy. Often they are attached to a Living Will (see below). Again, this appointment has no legal effect but it can be very useful if you would like your partner to make decisions regarding your treatment if you become incapable of doing so.

An Enduring Power of Attorney is another useful document for a patient to draw up because it creates a legal relationship which is binding on third parties. However, under an Enduring Power of Attorney, the attorney can only deal with the donor's property and affairs and cannot make decisions regarding the patient's medical care.

Living Wills

A patient who is suffering from a terminal illness can unwittingly cause disputes between relatives, partners, spouses, etc., and it is therefore often wise for them to make a Living Will. A Living Will is a statement about future medical treatment in the event that the patient becomes incapacitated. It can say in what circumstances a life support machine can be turned off and where the person would like to die (e.g. at home or in hospital). An example of a Law Pack Living Will is provided on the opposite page. Further information on Living Wills is provided in Law Pack's 'Enduring Power of Attorney & Living Wills' Guide.

Example Living Will

LIVING WILL

PERSONAL DETAILS

Name David Peter Ross

Address 5 Maple Terrace, London SW10 2FZ

Date of Birth 20 June 1935

Doctor's details Dr John Finlay 020 7111 2233

National Health Number 1234-56789

I, David Peter Ross , am of sound mind and make this Advance Directive now on my future medical care to my family, my doctors, other medical personnel and anyone else to whom it is relevant, for a time when, for reasons of physical or mental incapacity, I am unable to make my views known.

INSTRUCTIONS

Medical treatment I DO NOT want

I REFUSE medical procedures to prolong my life or keep me alive by artificial means if:-

(1) ~~I have a severe physical illness from which, in the opinion of~~ two ~~independent medical practitioners, it is unlikely that I will ever recover;~~ ☐

or

(2) I have a severe mental illness which, in the opinion of two independent medical practitioners, has no likelihood of improvement and in addition I have a severe physical illness from which, in the opinion of two independent medical practitioners, it is unlikely that I will ever recover; ☑

or

(3) I am permanently unconscious [and have been so for a period of at least 6 months] and [in the opinion of two independent medical practitioners] there is no likelihood that I will ever recover. ☑

Medical treatment I DO want

I DO wish to receive any medical treatment which will alleviate pain or distressing symptoms or will make me more comfortable. I accept that this may have the effect of shortening my life. ☑

~~[If I am suffering from any of the conditions above and I am pregnant, I wish to RECEIVE medical procedures which will prolong my life or keep me alive by artificial means only until such time as my child has been safely delivered.]~~

(Continued on next page)

Example Living Will (continued)

HEALTH CARE PROXY

I wish to appoint _____ Mrs. Gillian Ross _____ of _____
5 Maple Terrace, London SW10 2FZ as my Health Care Proxy. S/he should be involved in any decisions about my health care options if I am physically or mentally unable to make my views known. I wish to make it clear that s/he is fully aware of my wishes and I request that his/her decisions be respected.

ADDITIONAL DIRECTIONS ON FUTURE HEALTH CARE

None

SIGNATURES

Signature _David Ross_ Date _10 April 2001_

Witness' Signature _Thomas Waite_ Date _10 April 2001_

I confirm that my views are still as stated above.

	Date	Signature	Witness' Signature
1)			
2)			
3)			
4)			

© 1997 Law Pack Publishing Limited 10-16 Cole Street London SE1 4YH

70

Registration of death ━━━━━━

Under the Births and Deaths Registration Act 1953, only a 'qualified informant' can register a death. He can be:

i) a relative, present at the death or during the last illness; or failing that

ii) a relative, resident or present in the district in which the death occurred; or

iii) anybody present at the death or the occupier of the property if he knew of the death;

iv) any other person at the premises who knew of the death; or

v) anyone responsible for the disposal of the body.

If the death did not occur in a house then the duty to register the death falls, in order, upon:

i) any relative;

ii) anyone present at the death;

iii) anybody finding the body;

iv) anybody who deals with the disposal of the body.

Since a cohabitant is not a relative, according to the law, then the cohabitant may or may not be a qualified informant who is entitled to register the death.

Arranging a funeral

A cohabitant is entitled to dispose of the body of their partner if they are appointed executor under their partner's Will; but if their partner has died without a Will (i.e. intestate) or did not appoint the survivor as their executor under their Will, then there could be a conflict between their surviving partner and any other family members. This again shows how important it is that people who live together should execute Wills.

Remedies in the event of separation or death

If you and your partner separate, or if one of you dies, and you do not have a binding agreement regarding your financial arrangements, you may wish to consider the following legal remedies.

The Trusts of Land and Appointment of Trustees Act 1996

Under Section 14 of this Act, you can apply to a court for any property in which you and your partner have an interest to be sold or to prevent your partner from forcing a sale. When you go to court under this Section a court can also order that either you or your partner can be prevented from occupying the property and it can even order the person who stays in the property to pay compensation (which is sometimes called 'occupational rent') to the party who is excluded from it.

If it is not practicable to order one party to leave the property, then the court can partition the land or just order a sale of part of it, if that seems more appropriate.

When the court is considering whether or not to make an order under Section 14 of this Act, it has to take into account the following:

    i)   The intention of the people who own the property.

Therefore, if one person can show that the property was always intended to provide a home for the children of the family, the court may not order a sale until such time as the children are all grown up.

ii) The purpose for which the property was held.

Again, this could relate to either the property having been bought for the sake of the children or, alternatively, to house an elderly relative or for some other purpose.

iii) The welfare of any child who occupies or might be expected to occupy that property as their home.

If there are children involved, therefore, the court is less likely to order a sale although it might still order a sale in certain circumstances.

iv) The interests of any person who is owed money by an owner of the property who has registered the loan against the property.

This could include a building society who has a mortgage on the property which has not been paid and who wishes the property to be sold in order that the mortgage can be paid off.

As you will see therefore, the court is less likely to order a sale of the property where it is not in the interests of the children. However, this is not an overriding consideration and the court may therefore still order a sale even where there are children in certain circumstances.

Allowing someone else into the home

If your partner has allowed someone else into occupation of the property, then the law is very complex since the person they have allowed into the property is there with the permission of one owner but perhaps not with the permission of the other owner. They are not therefore guilty of trespass and usually, the only effective remedy of getting them out of the property is to force a sale. When you are drafting deeds of trust (see chapter 3), therefore, it is often a good idea to record that one person will not invite anybody else to occupy the property (e.g. a new boyfriend or girlfriend) without the agreement of the other partner, except in certain circumstances.

Schedule 1 of the Children Act

If you and your partner have a child/children and you separate, and the partner with whom the children are living does not have sufficient money either to house the children or to provide them with capital that the children desperately need (e.g. if they were handicapped – to convert the house), then that parent can apply for an order against the other parent either for a lump sum or for a property transfer order for the benefit of the child or children.

One of the most important distinctions between married couples and unmarried couples, however, is that if you are unmarried and have children, and you apply for an order under this Act, then any lump sum or capital that you receive as a result of an order made by the court will have to be given back to the parent against whom the order is made, usually once the child has reached 18 years of age or has finished their education. A spouse who receives a lump sum or a property transfer order in divorce proceedings does not usually have to pay it back.

Applications under Schedule 1 of the Children Act are often made by parents where the parent cannot adequately house the child of the relationship with the interest they have in the family home after they have calculated the value of their share in the property, either by using the equitable doctrines referred to in chapter 2 or in accordance with a trust deed or a Cohabitation Agreement they may have entered into. An application under Schedule 1 of the Children Act can therefore 'top-up' the monies or capital in a house that the parent looking after the children has so that they can provide a proper home for the children whilst the children are young.

In the recent case of P v. B (22 January 2001), a man retaliated against a mother who was making a successful claim against his property by cross-claiming damages under the tort of deceit on the basis that she had informed him that her child was his when paternity tests proved it was not. The court held he could pursue this claim although we are still waiting for the final hearing.

Negotiating a separation deed————

If your relationship breaks down and you do not wish to make an application to the court, and you do not have a binding Cohabitation Agreement or trust deed between you, then you could negotiate a deed between the two of you setting out the terms (including in particular the financial arrangements) of your separation. This deed will then form a binding contract between the two of you. It is therefore advisable that you take legal advice before entering into such a deed.

It can be expensive negotiating the terms of a deed between solicitors and, therefore, you may wish to consider attending mediation in order that you can negotiate the terms of your deed with a mediator. Mediation is a process whereby one mediator or, in certain circumstances, two mediators attempt to help you and your former partner to reach an agreement in relation to the issues that arise out of the breakdown of your relationship. It can therefore be used to cover both financial matters and issues concerning children. If you apply for public funding (which used to be called legal aid) then you will be asked to attend a mediation officer, prior to the issue of any public funding certificate so that the benefits of mediation can be explained to you. If you are interested in finding a mediator, then contact the UK College of Family Mediators (see Appendix 2).

Alternatively, if you wish to use a lawyer then it is always a good idea to contact a specialist family lawyer. The Solicitors Family Law Association is the largest Association representing family lawyers in the country and has approximately 5,000 members nationwide. All of the members subscribe to a Code of Conduct, the aim of which is to promote a conciliatory and amicable approach to issues arising out of the breakdown of a relationship. This approach is favoured by the court and is considered to be beneficial both to the family as a whole, particularly the children, and to keep costs to a minimum. If you wish to find the name and address of a member of the Solicitors Family Law Association in your area, then please contact the Administrative Director (see Appendix 2).

Death

In the event that your partner dies and there is no Will or you and/or the children have been left insufficient monies under your partner's Will, then you should consider making an application under the Inheritance (Provision for Family and Dependants) Act 1975. Children of the parent who has died are also entitled to make an application under this Act for provision out of their deceased parent's estate. If you are a cohabitant, you can make an application under this Act only if:

i)   you were financially dependant upon the deceased at the time of their death; and/or

ii) you have been living with the deceased for a continuous period of at least two years as husband and wife immediately prior to the date of death.

See chapter 7 for details relating to this.

As with separation, you are advised to take the advice of an Inheritance Act specialist if you are in this situation. Furthermore, if you find you are in a dispute with other members of the deceased's family it might be wise for you to consider reaching an agreement with them in mediation rather than going to court.

Take care on applications; under the Inheritance Act these *must* be made within six months of the grant of probate (if the deceased left a Will) or the 'grant of letters of administration' (if the deceased died intestate). It is difficult to extend this time limit, so do ensure any application under this Act is made without delay.

Appendices

Appendix 1: Sources of documents

Cohabitation Agreement	Draft your own based on the example in this Guide
Enduring Power of Attorney	Legal stationers
Health Care Proxy	Your local hospital
Last Will & Testament	Law Pack F216 Form available via **www.lawpack.co.uk** or call 020 7940 7000
Living Together Agreement	Draft your own based on example in this Guide
Living Will	Law Pack F212 Form available via **www.lawpack.co.uk** or call 020 7940 7000
Non-Molestation and Occupation Order, FL401	Court Service website **www.courtservice.gov.uk** or call 020 7947 6000
Parental Responsibility Agreement, C(PRA)	Court Service website **www.courtservice.gov.uk** or call 020 7947 6000
Trust Deed	Your conveyancing solicitor

Appendix 2: Useful contacts

Name	Address
HM Land Charges Registry *(unregistered land)*	Drakes Hill Court Burrington Way Plymouth PL5 3LP Tel: 01752 635600
HM Land Registry *(registered land)*	32 Lincoln's Inn Fields London WC2A 3PH Tel: 020 7917 8888 www.landreg.gov.uk
Law Society	113 Chancery Lane London WC2A 1PL Tel: 020 7242 1222 www.lawsociety.org.uk
National Association of Citizens Advice Bureaux	115 Pentonville Road London N1 9LZ Tel: 020 7833 2181 www.nacab.org.uk
National Council for One Parent Families	255 Kentish Town Road London NW5 1TL Tel: 020 7428 5400 www.oneparentfamilies.org.uk
National Family & Parenting Institute	430 Highgate Studios 53–79 Highgate Road London NW5 1TL Tel: 020 7424 3460 www.nfpi.org
Principal Registry of the Family Division	The Children's Section (Room 2.11) 1st Avenue 42–49 High Holborn London WC1V 6NP Tel: 020 7947 7461/6939
Relate	Herbert Gray College Little Church Street Rugby CV21 3AP Tel 01788 573241 www.relate.org.uk

Solicitors Family Law
Association
(*for solicitors and mediators*)

PO Box 302
Orpington BR6 8QX
Tel: 01689 850227
www.sfla.co.uk

UK College of
Family Mediators

24–32 Stephenson Way
London NW1 2HX
Tel: 020 7391 9162
www.ukcfm.co.uk

Index

This index covers the Introduction and chapters, but not appendices.
An 'e' after a page number indicates an example, or example and text.

abduction, children 42
associated couples 49-50

bank accounts, joint 36-7e
Births and Deaths Registration
      Act (1953) 71

Child Abduction Act (1984) 42
Child Support Agency 21
children 28e, 39 see also parents
      abduction 42
      age
            and consideration of
            views 40
            and medical
            responsibility 40
      contact orders 41
      false paternity case 75
      financial contributions for,
      on separation 21, 75
      mediation for 4
      prohibited steps orders 41
      and property 74, 75
      residence orders 41
      specific issue orders 41-2

surnames, Parental
      Responsibility Agreements
      44-5
Children Act (1989) 39, 75
      principle of no order 40
Cohabitation Agreements 2, 23,
      32-8e
      complicated 30
      financial contributions 27,
      30
      limitations 53-4, 55
      simple 27, 30
      timing 3
      updating 3, 30-1
      upholding 3
commitment in relationships, and
      occupation orders 51
common law married couples
      ix-x
consideration 28e
constructive trusts
      agreements 13-14
      financial contributions, non-
      structural 14
contact orders, children 41

death
    registration 71
    survivors, funds
    applications 77
deeds of trust 9-10, 23-6e
Denning, Baron Alfred
    Thompson 8
doctrine of necessity 68

Enduring Power of Attorney 62-
    4e
    costs 61e
    gifts 65-6
    liabilities 60, 65
    limitations 59, 61e, 65, 68
    powers 60, 61e, 65
    registration 61e
    regulations 61e
    steps 66-7
Enduring Powers of Attorney Act
    (1985) 59
engaged couples 7
    Pre-nuptial Agreements 31
equitable accounting
    disadvantages 15e
    financial contributions, on
    separation 15-16e, 17e
    mortgages 16e
equity 8
exclusion zones, occupation
    orders 50
express trusts 9-10

families 28e
Family Law Act (1996) 49
Financial Agreements *see*
    Cohabitation Agreements
funerals 71
    Wills, directions in 56e

gifts 20, 37e
    from Enduring Power of
    Attorney 65-6

in Wills 55, 56e

harassment 52
health and safety issues,
    occupation orders 51
health care proxies 68, 70e
history ix-x
homosexual couples 49-50
housework 29e
housing needs, occupation orders
    50-1

income 20-1
inequalities see married couples,
    inequalities vs.
Inheritance (Provision for Family
    and Dependants) Act (1975)
    53, 57, 77
insurance policies 33e
intestacy 53-5

joint tenancies 9-10, 24 see also
    severance

Land Registry 20, 23-4
Living Together Agreements 1-
    2, 28-9e
    non-legal issues 26-7e
    non-legal restrictions 27e
Living Wills 68-70e

M
maintenance payments 20-1
Marriage Act (1753) x
married couples, inequalities vs.
    ix, 1, 7
    children, financial
    contributions for, on
    separation 75
    funerals 71
    intestacy 53-5
    mental capacity, failing 59
    occupation orders 50

redress from 8
Wills 53
Matrimonial Causes Act (1973)
7
mediation 76
benefits 5-6
for children 4
confidentiality 5
in finances 4
neutrality 4-5
in separation 4
with solicitors 4
medical intervention
choices 69e
uncertainties 67-8
medical responsibility, children,
age and 40
mental capacity
failing 59, 60
and power of attorney see
Enduring Power of Attorney
soundness of mind 57
molestation 49, 50
mortgages 10-11e
endowment 12e
equitable accounting 16e

next of kin, uncertainties 67-8
non-molestation orders 49, 50

occupation orders
applicants 50
behavioural issues 51
and commitment in
relationships 51
conditions 51-2
exclusion zones 50
financial needs 51, 52
health and safety issues 51
housing needs 50-1
openness 28e
outside interests 28e
ownership

beneficial 8
equitable accounting 15-
17e
joint tenancies 9-10, 24
see also severance
proprietary estoppel 14-
15e
tenancies in common 9,
24, 26 see also
severance
trusts for see trust
entries
legal 8
property see property

Parental Responsibility
Agreements 46-7e
allocations 43
children's surnames 44-5
duration 43
identification for 44
registration 45
signatories 43-4
witnessing 45
parents 28e see also children
false paternity case 75
informal negotiations 42
responsibility 42
allocation 40, 43
possessions
joint 37e
personal 20, 38e
power of attorney see Enduring
Power of Attorney
Pre-nuptial Agreements 31
prohibited steps orders, children
41
property 8
additional occupants 36e,
74-5
buying 36e
children and 74, 75
division 73-5

equitable accounting 15-17e
ex-council 12
financial contributions
non-structural 12e, 14, 33-4e
structural 12e, 15-16e, 17e, 33-5e
housing needs 50-1
improvements 34-5e
insurance policies 33e
intended purposes 73-4
joint tenancies 9-10, 24
Land Registry 20, 23-4
mortgages 10-11e
endowment 12e
equitable accounting and 16e
obsolescent laws 3
occupation orders 50-2
outstanding interests 74
proprietary estoppel 14-15e
purchasing 32e
selling 35-6e
severance 17-20e
in sole name 23
tenancies in common 9, 24, 26
trusts for *see trust entries*
Wills and 9
proprietary estoppel
disadvantages 15e
mistaken beliefs 14-15e
Protection from Harassment Act (1996) 52

residence orders, children 41
resulting trusts
disadvantages 12-13e
financial contributions 10
non-structural 12e
structural 12e

mortgages 10-12e
rights, lack of *see* married couples, inequalities vs.

separation
children in *see* children
deeds for 76
mediation in 4
property division 73-5
severance 17-20e *see also* joint tenancies; tenancies in common
solicitors, with mediation 4
Solicitors Family Law Association 76
soundness of mind 57
specific issue orders, children 41-2

tenancies in common 9, 24, 26
see also severance
Trusts of Land and Appointment of Trustees Act (1996) 73-4

unawareness ix, 12e
uncertainties x
medical intervention 67-8
next of kin 67-8

Wills 53, 71
contesting 57
executors 56e
funerals, directions for 56e
gifts in 55, 56e
omissions, explaining 57
prerequisites 55
property and 9
soundness of mind 57

Notes

Notes

Law Pack tenancy and other Form Packs...

England and Wales Form Packs

Furnished House or Flat Rental Agreement
(on an Assured Shorthold Tenancy)

Code F201 • £4.49 • ISBN 1 902646 09 6

Unfurnished House or Flat Rental Agreement
(on an Assured Shorthold Tenancy)

Code F202 • £4.49 • ISBN 1 902646 10 X

House or Flat Share Agreement
(for a room in a furnished house or flat with a resident owner)

Code F203 • £4.49 • ISBN 1 902646 08 8

House or Flat Share Agreement
(for a room in a furnished house or flat with a non-resident owner)

Code F204 • £4.49 • ISBN 1 902646 07 X

Holiday Letting Agreement
(for holiday lets of furnished property)

Code F213 • £4.49 • ISBN 1 898217 53 X

Notice to Terminate
(for use with either Rental or House/Flat Share Agreements)

Code F206 • £4.49 • ISBN 1 902646 12 6

Rent Book
(records rent paid – required by law if rent is paid weekly)

Code F207 • £4.49 • ISBN 1 898217 27 0

Household Inventory

Code F208 • £4.49 • ISBN 1 898217 32 7

Last Will & Testament (for gifts not in trust)

Code F216 • £4.49 • ISBN 1 902646 14 2

General Power of Attorney (to authorise another to act on your behalf with full legal authority)

Code F220 • £4.49 • ISBN 1 902646 16 9

Living Will
(your advance instructions on medical treatment)

Code F212 • £4.49 • ISBN 1 898217 52 1

Cohabitation Agreement (for unmarried partners)

Code F217 • £4.49 • ISBN 1 898217 73 4

Employment Contract
(standard agreement between employer and employee)

Code F209 • £4.49 • ISBN 1 902646 11 8

Builder/Decorator Contract
(details work to be done, time-scale, payment etc.)

Code F210 • £4.49 • ISBN 1 898217 42 4

Business Partnership Agreement
(contract between individuals starting partnership)

Code F211 • £4.49 • ISBN 1 902646 15 0

Sales Representative Agreement
(sets out products, territory, commission etc.)

Code F218 • £4.49 • ISBN 1 898217 78 5

Anti-Gazumping Agreement
(for exclusivity before exchange when buying property)

Code F214 • £4.49 • ISBN 1 898217 58 0

Pools Syndicate Agreement
(safeguards any winnings of group football pools players)

Code F219 • £4.49 • ISBN 1 898217 83 1

Vehicle Purchase Agreement
(for private sale of car, van or motorcycle)

Code F221 • £4.49 • ISBN 1 902646 31 2

National Lottery Syndicate Agreement
(safeguards any winnings of group Lottery players)

Code J215 • £4.49 • ISBN 1 898217 93 9

... to order, simply call 020 7940 7000 or visit www.lawpack.co.uk

More books from Law Pack...

Motoring Law

Whether we like it or not, motoring is fact of everyday life. But how many drivers actually know their rights and those of the police? The Highway Code provides the driving basics. This Law Pack Guide is essential follow-up reading on the motorist's real rights and remedies.

Code B415 • ISBN 1 898217 51 3 • A4 PB
104 pp • £9.99 • 1st Edition

Credit File

Refused credit? Bad credit? We nearly all rely on credit, whether it be with the bank, mortgage lender or credit card company. This Law Pack Guide explains just how credit agencies work, what goes on to your credit file and what legitimate action you can take to improve it. It divulges lenders decision-making processes and blows the lid off 'credit repair' and credit 'blacklists'.

Code B413 • ISBN 1 898217 77 7 • A4 pb
76 pp • £9.99 • 1st Edition

House Buying, Selling and Conveyancing

It isn't true that only those who have gone through long, expensive and involved training can possibly understand the intricacies of house buying, selling and conveyancing. This Law Pack Guide is a new, updated edition of a best-selling book by Joseph Bradshaw, once described in *The Times* as the 'guru of layperson conveyancing', which explains step-by-step just how straightforward the whole process really is. Required reading for all house buyers (or sellers).

Code B412 • ISBN 1 898712 72 6 • A4 PB
192pp • £9.99 • 1st Edition

... to order, simply call 020 7940 7000 or visit www.lawpack.co.uk

Probate

What happens when someone dies, with or without leaving a Will, and their estate needs to be dealt with? Probate is the process whereby the deceased's executors apply for authority to handle the deceased's assets. This Guide provides the information and instructions needed to obtain a grant of probate, or grant of letters of administration, and administer an estate without the expense of a solicitor.

Code B409 • ISBN 1 902646 27 4 • 246 x 189mm
96 pp • £9.99 • 2nd Edition

Divorce

File your own undefended divorce and save legal fees! This Guide explains the process from filing your petition to final decree. Even if there are complications such as young children or contested grounds this Guide will save you time and money.

Code B404 • ISBN 1 902646 05 3 • A4 PB
120 pp • £9.99 • 2nd Edition

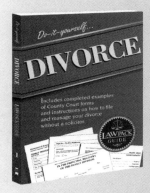

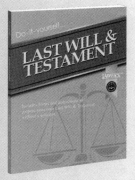

Last Will & Testament

With the help of this Guide writing a Will can be a straightforward matter. It takes the reader step by step through the process of drawing up a Will, while providing background information and advice. Will forms, completed examples and checklists included.

Code B403 • ISBN 1 902646 06 1 • A4 PB
80 pp • £9.99 • 2nd Edition

... to order, simply call 020 7940 7000 or visit www.lawpack.co.uk

Small Claims

If you want to take action to recover a debt, resolve a contract dispute or make a personal injury claim, you can file your own small claim without a solicitor. This Guide includes clear instructions and advice on how to handle your own case and enforce judgment.

Code B406 • ISBN 1 902646 04 5 • A4 PB
96 pp • £9.99 • 2nd Edition

Personnel Manager

A Form Book of more than 200 do-it-yourself forms, contracts and letters to help you manage your personnel needs more effectively. As employment laws and codes of practice increasingly affect the workplace, good, efficient record-keeping is essential for any employer, large or small. There's no quicker or easier way to 'get it in writing' than using *Personnel Manager*. Areas covered: Recruitment & Hiring, Employment Contracts & Agreements, Handling New Employees, Personnel Management, Performance Evaluation and Termination of Employment.

Code B417 • ISBN 1 902646 02 9 • A4 PB
246 pp • £19.99 • 2nd Edition

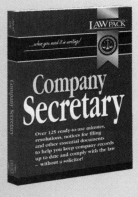

Company Secretary

What every busy company secretary or record-keeper needs. Maintaining good, up-to-date records of company meetings and resolutions is not only good practice but also a legal requirement, however small your company is. This Form Book makes compiling minutes of board and shareholder meetings straightforward. It includes more than 125 commonly-required resolutions and minutes: all that a limited company is likely to need.

Code B416 • ISBN 1 902646 19 3 • A4 PB
190 pp • £19.99 • 2nd Edition

... to order, simply call 020 7940 7000 or visit www.lawpack.co.uk